OPENING *Intuition* **BOOK 1**

PSYCHIC DEVELOPMENT
THE BASICS

AN EASY-TO-USE, STEP-BY-STEP ILLUSTRATED G

LUCY BYATT   **KIM ROBERTS**

FINDHORN PRESS

OPENING 2intuition

PUBLISHED IN 2016 BY FINDHORN PRESS, SCOTLAND
ISBN 978-1-84409-702-9

PROOFREAD BY NICKY LEACH
DESIGN BY LUCY BYATT
PRINTED AND BOUND IN THE EU

PUBLISHED BY FINDHORN PRESS
DELFT COTTAGE, DYKE,
FORRES IV36 2TF,
SCOTLAND, UK
TEL +44(0)1309-690582
FAX +44(0)131-777-2711
FINDHORNPRESS.COM
INFO@FINDHORNPRESS.COM

DISCLAIMER

OPENING2INTUITION, LUCY BYATT &
KIM ROBERTS, OFFER THEIR WORK FOR
YOUR PLEASURE & ENTERTAINMENT. AS
ARTISTS & CREATORS, WE BELIEVE THAT
THROUGH OUR OWN EXPERIENCES OUR
IDEAS ARE WORTHY OF PUBLICATION
& PRESENTATION. WE ADVISE YOU NOT
TO USE THIS WORK AS AN ALTERNATIVE
TO PRACTICAL MEDICINE OR MENTAL
& EMOTIONAL HEALTH CARE. WE ALSO
SUGGEST YOU DO NOT DRIVE DURING
OR IMMEDIATELY AFTER DOING ANY
OF THESE EXERCISES. HOWEVER WE
DO URGE YOU TO ENJOY, EXPAND AND
BECOME CONSCIOUS OF THE BEAUTIFUL
SPIRIT THAT YOU TRULY ARE.

CONTENTS

WE RECOMMEND YOU USE THE COMPANION
OPENING2INTUITION STARTER AUDIO-CD
WHEN YOU PRACTISE THE EXERCISES AND
VISUALIZATIONS DESCRIBED IN THIS GUIDEBOOK.

TRACK 1
TRACK 3
TRACK 4
TRACK 2
TRACK 8
TRACK 5

TIP:

ALL TEMPLATES IN THIS BOOK,
AS WELL AS IN BOOKS 2 AND 3, CAN BE
DOWNLOADED IN ONE GO AT
ganxy.com/i/111812

STARTER AUDIO-CD

HERE AT OPENING2INTUITION WE AIM TO PROVIDE A TEACHING PLATFORM THAT IS ACCESSIBLE TO EVERYONE. WE WANT TO MAKE DEVELOPING YOUR INTUITION EASY, FUN AND SAFE. THIS IS WHY WE HAVE DEVELOPED AN ACCOMPANYING CD FOR THIS BOOK. NOW YOU CAN DO ALL OF OUR MEDITATIONS LISTENING TO THIS CD. JUST SIT DOWN, RELAX AND BE GUIDED ON SOME FANTASTIC VISUALIZATIONS.

 OPENING UP

 CLEARING YOUR ENERGY

 PROTECTION (BUBBLE)

 PROTECTION (CLOAK/ARMOUR)

 GROUNDING

TRACK 6 **MEETING YOUR SPIRIT GUIDE**

TRACK 7 **PAST LIFE VISUALIZATION**

TRACK 8 **CLOSING DOWN**

THE OPENING2INTUITION STARTER AUDIO-CD WAS DEVELOPED BY OURSELVES WITH MUSICIAN AND SOUND HEALER KAREN GRACE. KAREN HAS WORKED IN SOUND HEALING FOR A NUMBER OF YEARS. SHE HAS USED HER KNOWLEDGE OF SOUND VIBRATION AND THE EFFECTS THAT SOUND HAS ON OUR ENERGY FIELD TO RECORD THIS CD.

THE SOUNDS THEMSELVES ARE DESIGNED TO TAKE YOU DEEPER, AND TO OPEN YOUR ENERGETIC FIELD IN NEW WAYS. YOU CAN USE THIS CD TO TAKE YOUR INTUITIVE PRACTICE ONE STEP FURTHER.

OPENING2INTUITION STARTER CD IS AVAILABLE FROM YOUR LOCAL BOOKSHOP OR FROM

WWW.FINDHORNPRESS.COM

WHERE YOU WILL ALSO FIND A DOWNLOADABLE MP3 VERSION.

OPENING 2 intuition

OUR INTENTION AT **OPENING2INTUITION** IS TO PROVIDE A SAFE AND SIMPLE WAY FOR PEOPLE TO OPEN UP TO THEIR INTUITIVE SELF. WE BELIEVE THAT EVERYONE CAN BE INTUITIVE AND DEVELOP THEIR PSYCHIC AND HEALING ABILITIES. IN FACT, THE PROCESS IS VERY SIMPLE AND NOT COMPLICATED AT ALL.

AT **OPENING2INTUITION** WE HAVE DEVELOPED A VISUAL PROCESS OF LEARNING THAT ALLOWS YOU TO SEE HOW ENERGY WORKS. THIS BOOK IS THE FOUNDATION OF A SERIES OF BOOKS THAT STARTS WITH THE BASICS AND DEVELOP WITH EACH VOLUME. OUR AIM IS TO MAKE INTUITIVE WORK AVAILABLE TO EVERYONE AND TO TEACH IN WAYS THAT TARGET EVERYONE'S INDIVIDUAL LEARNING CAPABILITIES. ENERGY WORK IS NOT ALWAYS EASY TO UNDERSTAND. SOME PEOPLE DON'T NECESSARILY SEE THE ENERGIES AT WORK IN THE WORLD THAT PSYCHIC AND INTUITIVE PEOPLE ACCESS. THIS IS WHY WE HAVE CHOSEN TO MAKE THIS BOOK A VISUAL BOOK. WE WANT TO SHOW YOU HOW ENERGY WORKS, HOW VARIOUS PSYCHIC DEVELOPMENT EXERCISES WORK AND WHAT ACTUALLY HAPPENS WITH ENERGY WHEN YOU OPEN UP INTUITIVELY.

OPENING UP TO YOUR INTUITION SHOULD BE FUN. WITH THIS BOOK YOU CAN WORK AT YOUR OWN PACE, LEARNING THROUGH EACH OF THE CHAPTERS, BUILDING YOUR SKILLS. IT STARTS WITH THE BASICS AND DEVELOPS YOUR KNOWLEDGE THE FURTHER YOU GO THROUGH THE BOOK. THERE IS ALSO AN ACCOMPANYING CD DESIGNED AROUND THE EXERCISES IN THIS BOOK. THE CD HAS BEEN CO-CREATED WITH MUSICIAN, HEALER AND PSYCHIC, KAREN GRACE. THE CD USES SPECIFIC SOUND VIBRATIONS TO OPEN AND EXPAND YOUR INTUITION IN NEW WAYS.

YOU CAN ALSO VISIT OUR WEBSITE TO LEARN MORE ABOUT OUR UPCOMING BOOKS, CDS AND TEACHING COURSES.

WWW.OPENING2INTUITION.COM

Kim Roberts and Lucy Byatt
X

INTRODUCTION

OPENING2INTUITION WELCOMES YOU TO THE FIRST GUIDEBOOK IN A SERIES OF PSYCHIC AND SPIRITUAL DEVELOPMENT BOOKS.

IT WILL TEACH YOU HOW ENERGY WORKS IN YOUR BODY THROUGH YOUR CHAKRAS, AS WELL AS IN THE WORLD ALL AROUND YOU.

THIS OUR FIRST BOOK. IT FOCUSES ON DEVELOPING BASIC PSYCHIC DEVELOPMENT TECHNIQUES.

IT IS DESIGNED AS A SIMPLE STEP-BY-STEP GUIDEBOOK,

REVEALING THE PROCESS OF HOW WE CAN OPEN TO OUR OWN INTUITION.

THROUGHOUT THIS BOOK, YOU WILL LEARN ABOUT ENERGY,

HOW TO WORK WITH IT, CLEANSE IT AND USE IT.

ZZZT

TOO MUCH ENERGY!!!!

IT CONSISTS OF A SERIES OF EXERCISES THAT YOU WILL BE ABLE TO READ ABOUT, THEN FOLLOW, STEP BY STEP.

OVER THE COURSE OF WORKING THROUGH THE BOOK, YOU WILL BEGIN TO RECORD YOUR OWN REACTIONS AND WAYS THAT YOU WORK INTUITIVELY.

CHECK-IN ACTIVITIES:

EVERYTHING ABOUT THIS BOOK IS ABOUT YOU WORKING AT YOUR OWN PACE.

THROUGHOUT THE **OPENING2INTUITION** BOOKS THERE ARE CHECK-IN POINTS THAT ARE DESIGNED TO HELP YOU TO COLLECT INFORMATION AND RECORD YOUR EXPERIENCES.

SLOWLY BUILDING YOUR KNOWLEDGE AND DISCOVERING HOW YOU WORK AS AN INTUITIVE ENERGY WORKER.

IT'S TIME TO ENJOY LEARNING HOW TO OPEN TO YOUR INTUITION!

INTRODUCTION

THE BASICS

FIRST THINGS FIRST

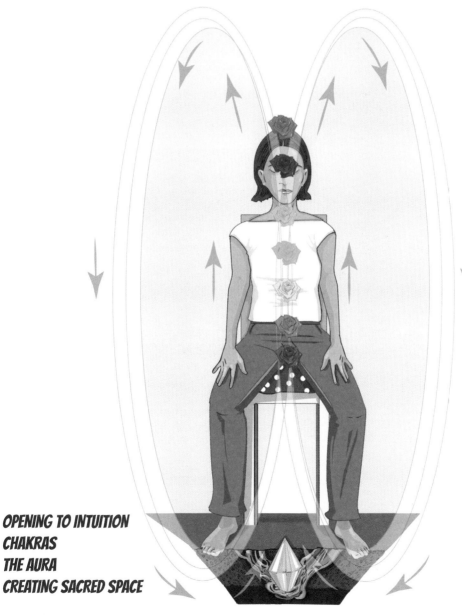

OPENING TO INTUITION
CHAKRAS
THE AURA
CREATING SACRED SPACE

OPENING UP
CLOSING DOWN
GROUNDING

OPENING TO INTUITION

OPENING TO INTUITION IS THE PROCESS OF OPENING YOUR MIND AND YOUR ENERGY SYSTEM. THIS ENABLES YOU TO TUNE INTO THE ENERGIES AROUND YOU.

YOUR INTUITION IS THE PART OF YOU THAT INSTINCTUALLY KNOWS OR SENSES THINGS, WITHOUT THE USE OF RATIONAL THOUGHT.

IT IS THE GUT FEELING THAT YOU MIGHT HAVE ABOUT SOMETHING.

DON'T LEAVE MOUSIE. I DON'T FEEL IT'S SAFE OUT THERE!!!

NONSENSE! I'VE BEEN OUT THERE HUNDREDS OF TIMES, AND NOTHING HAS EVER HAPPENED!

IT IS THE INTUITIVE SENSE OF KNOWING SOMETHING WILL OCCUR PRIOR TO IT OCCURRING.

WHEN WE BEGIN TO EXPLORE OUR PSYCHIC ABILITIES

THE STARTING POINT IS OUR INTUITION. IT WILL BE THROUGH OUR INTUITION THAT WE WILL DISCOVER THE PSYCHIC IN US.

I CAN SEE!!!!

THIS INTUITIVE PART OF WHO WE ARE WILL OPEN US UP TO NEW SENSATIONS, FEELINGS AND OUR CLAIRVOYANT VISION.

IT IS THROUGH TUNING INTO OUR OWN INNER FEELINGS ABOUT THE PEOPLE AND PLACES AROUND US THAT WE ARE ABLE TO BEGIN TO READ THE WORLD OF ENERGY.

ENERGY IN THE WORLD

EVERYTHING AROUND US IS MADE UP OF ENERGY.

WE EACH HAVE AN ENERGETIC VIBRATION WE SEND OUT TO THE WORLD.

THIS ENERGY VIBRATION CHANGES DEPENDING ON HOW WE MAY FEEL AT ANY PARTICULAR MOMENT.

POSITIVE

NEGATIVE

LISTEN TO YOUR FATHER

nothing ever works !

THESE VIBRATIONS WILL BE PICKED UP BY OTHER PEOPLE. THEY WILL SENSE THE MOOD OF THE PERSON, JUST THROUGH THE ENERGY THAT THEY ARE EMITTING.

PLACES AROUND US EACH CARRY THEIR OWN UNIQUE VIBRATIONS.

VIBRATION CAN BE PICKED UP BY PEOPLE WHO ARE VISITING THAT PLACE.

A BATTLEFIELD MAY HOLD THE EMOTIONAL MEMORIES OF THE PAST.

A PLACE WITH A LOT OF HISTORY CAN HOLD ONTO THE ENERGY OF EVENTS THAT OCCURRED THERE.

HURRY ALONG NOW, ALGERNON, OR YOU'LL MISS THIS SENSATIONAL VIEW!

WHEN A HIGHLY SENSITIVE PERSON STEPS OUT INTO THIS FIELD, THEY COULD QUICKLY PICK UP THE NEGATIVE FEELINGS ASSOCIATED WITH THE HISTORY OF THE PLACE.

THIS CAN ALSO WORK IN THE OPPOSITE WAY, AS IN THE BELL ROCK VORTEX IN SEDONA.

BELL ROCK

BELL ROCK, ARIZONA IS A KNOWN VORTEX SPOT AND HAS A VERY POSITIVE AND UPLIFTING ENERGY TO THOSE PEOPLE ENTERING ITS SPACE.

AS WELL AS PLACES AND PEOPLE, OBJECTS THEMSELVES HOLD THEIR OWN VIBRATION.

A PSYCHIC CAN USE A TECHNIQUE LIKE PSYCHOMETRY TO READ THE ENERGY OF AN OBJECT.

THIS OCCURS BECAUSE WE LEAVE AN ENERGY IMPRINT OF OURSELVES IN OBJECTS AND THIS CAN EASILY BE READ BY A PSYCHIC.

CHAKRAS

CHAKRAS AND OUR ENERGY SYSTEM

OUR ENERGY SYSTEM IS MADE UP OF A COLLECTION OF SEVEN DIFFERENT ENERGY CENTRES, CALLED CHAKRAS. THESE SEVEN CHAKRAS ARE LOCATED ALONG THE SPINE. THEY START WITH THE BASE CHAKRA IN THE PELVIS AND MOVE UP THE SPINE, ENDING WITH THE CROWN CHAKRA AT THE TOP OF THE HEAD.

CROWN

THIRD EYE

THROAT

EACH CHAKRA REPRESENTS A PART OF THE BODY. HOW EACH CHAKRA FLOWS AT THAT TIME REFLECTS THE PERSON'S EMOTIONAL AND SPIRITUAL HEALTH.

HEART

A CHAKRA IS AN ENERGY CENTRE AND CAN BE LIKENED TO A SPINNING VORTEX.

SOLAR

SACRAL

BASE

THE SEVEN CHAKRAS RUN ALONG THE SPINE, STARTING AT THE PELVIS WITH THE BASE CHAKRA, ENDING AT THE CROWN CHAKRA ABOVE THE HEAD.

EACH INDIVIDUAL CHAKRA HAS A PARTICULAR FUNCTION.

EACH CHAKRA IS CONNECTED TO AN AREA OF THE BODY AND THE EMOTIONS THAT RELATE TO IT.

BASE

THE BASE CHAKRA IS LOCATED AT THE BASE OF THE SPINE. THIS CHAKRA IS REPRESENTED BY THE COLOUR RED. IT IS LINKED TO OUR PHYSICAL WELL-BEING AND OUR SENSE OF SUPPORT AND STABILITY IN LIFE. PHYSICALLY IT CONTROLS THE LOWER BODY, LEGS AND FEET. EMOTIONALLY IT IS LINKED TO OUR SENSE OF STABILITY AND HOW GROUNDED AND SAFE WE FEEL IN THE WORLD. IT IS CONNECTED TO OUR PRIMAL SELF AND OUR SURVIVAL AND SELF-ESTEEM.

WHEN THE BASE CHAKRA IS BALANCED, AN INDIVIDUAL WILL FEEL GROUNDED, SUPPORTED AND STRONG IN THEIR SENSE OF SELF. WHEN IT IS OUT OF BALANCE, THE INDIVIDUAL WILL FEEL UNGROUNDED AND UNSUPPORTED.

SACRAL

THE SACRAL CHAKRA IS THE SECOND CHAKRA, JUST BELOW THE NAVEL, REPRESENTED BY THE COLOUR ORANGE. IT IS LINKED TO OUR CREATIVITY, FERTILITY AND PERSONAL RELATIONSHIPS. PHYSICALLY IT CONTROLS THE SEXUAL ORGANS, STOMACH, INTESTINES, LIVER AND PANCREAS.

EMOTIONALLY THIS CHAKRA LINKS TO OUR CREATIVE EXPRESSION AND OUR PERSONAL RELATIONSHIPS WITH FAMILY, PARTNERS AND FRIENDS.

SOLAR PLEXUS

THE SOLAR PLEXUS IS THE THIRD CHAKRA, FOUND IN THE CENTRE OF THE RIBS. THIS CHAKRA IS REPRESENTED BY THE COLOUR YELLOW. IT IS LINKED TO OUR SENSE OF PERSONAL POWER AND EGO. PHYSICALLY IT CONTROLS THE ADRENALS, INTESTINES AND THE GALL BLADDER. EMOTIONALLY IT REPRESENTS OUR SENSE OF POWER AND HOW EMPOWERED WE FEEL WITHIN OURSELVES.

WHEN AN INDIVIDUAL HAS A BALANCED SOLAR PLEXUS CHAKRA, THEY ARE SELF-ASSURED AND STAND IN THEIR OWN POWER WITH EASE. WHEN THIS CHAKRA IS PUT OUT OF BALANCE, THE INDIVIDUAL MAY FEEL NERVOUS, ANXIOUS AND UNSURE OF THEIR PLACE IN THE WORLD.

HEART

THE HEART CHAKRA IS LOCATED IN THE HEART. REPRESENTED BY THE COLOUR GREEN IT IS LINKED TO THE HEART AND CONNECTS TO OUR SENSE OF COMPASSION AND LOVE.

WHEN SOMEONE HAS A BALANCED HEART CHAKRA THEY WILL SHOW COMPASSION AND LOVE WITH EASE. IF IT IS CLOSED THE PERSON COULD HAVE PROBLEMS WITH FEAR AROUND RELATIONSHIPS. THEY MAY FIND IT HARD TO OPEN UP AND EXPRESS THEIR EMOTIONS AND FEELINGS.

THROAT

THE THROAT CHAKRA IS LOCATED IN THE THROAT. REPRESENTED BY THE COLOUR BLUE IT IS LINKED TO THE VOICE, THE THROAT AND HOW WE ARE ABLE TO COMMUNICATE AND SPEAK OUR OWN TRUTH.

WHEN THIS CHAKRA IS IN BALANCE THE PERSON WILL BE ABLE TO COMMUNICATE FREELY. THEY ARE ABLE TO SPEAK THEIR TRUTH AND EXPRESS THEMSELVES CREATIVELY. WHEN THE CHAKRA IS BLOCKED THE PERSON MAY FIND IT HARD TO COMMUNICATE AND BE OPEN WITH THEIR CREATIVITY.

THIRD EYE

THE THIRD EYE IS LOCATED IN THE CENTRE OF THE BROW. IREPRESENTED BY A DEEP BLUE PURPLE COLOUR. IT IS LINKED TO OUR INTUITION AND WISDOM, AND PHYSICALLY TO THE BRAIN AND EYES.

WHEN THIS CHAKRA IS IN BALANCE THE INDIVIDUAL WILL BE OPEN TO THEIR INTUITION AND OWN INNER WISDOM. WHEN THIS CHAKRA IS OUT OF BALANCE, THE PERSON MAY FEEL CONFUSED AND DOUBTFUL AROUND THEIR OWN INTUITION FINDING IT HARD TO SEE THINGS CLEARLY.

CROWN

THE CROWN CHAKRA IS LOCATED AT THE TOP OF THE HEAD. IT IS LINKED TO THE COLOURS WHITE AND VIOLET AND TO OUR SPIRITUAL CONNECTION WITH THE UNIVERSE AND PHYSICALLY TO THE BRAIN AND PINEAL GLAND.

WHEN THIS CHAKRA IS IN BALANCE, THE PERSON WILL FEEL CONNECTED TO THEIR SPIRITUALITY AND UNIVERSAL CONNECTION. WHEN THIS CHAKRA IS OUT OF BALANCE, AN INDIVIDUAL WILL FEEL DISCONNECTED FROM THEIR SPIRITUALITY AND CONNECTION TO THE WORLD.

THE AURA

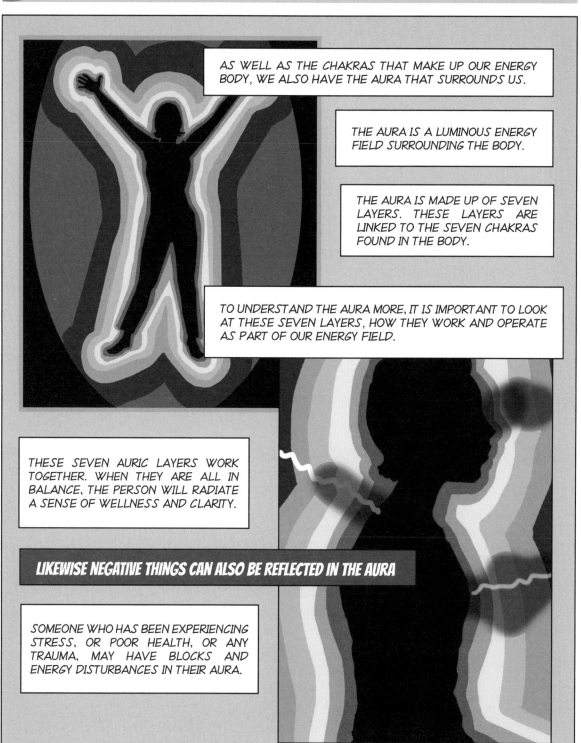

AS WELL AS THE CHAKRAS THAT MAKE UP OUR ENERGY BODY, WE ALSO HAVE THE AURA THAT SURROUNDS US.

THE AURA IS A LUMINOUS ENERGY FIELD SURROUNDING THE BODY.

THE AURA IS MADE UP OF SEVEN LAYERS. THESE LAYERS ARE LINKED TO THE SEVEN CHAKRAS FOUND IN THE BODY.

TO UNDERSTAND THE AURA MORE, IT IS IMPORTANT TO LOOK AT THESE SEVEN LAYERS, HOW THEY WORK AND OPERATE AS PART OF OUR ENERGY FIELD.

THESE SEVEN AURIC LAYERS WORK TOGETHER. WHEN THEY ARE ALL IN BALANCE, THE PERSON WILL RADIATE A SENSE OF WELLNESS AND CLARITY.

LIKEWISE NEGATIVE THINGS CAN ALSO BE REFLECTED IN THE AURA

SOMEONE WHO HAS BEEN EXPERIENCING STRESS, OR POOR HEALTH, OR ANY TRAUMA, MAY HAVE BLOCKS AND ENERGY DISTURBANCES IN THEIR AURA.

THE LAYERS OF THE AURAS

1 THE ETHERIC LAYER

1 - 2 INCHES

← — — — —

2 - 5 CENTIMETERS

THE ETHERIC LAYER IS THE LAYER OF THE AURA THAT IS CLOSEST TO THE BODY. IT EXPANDS 1 TO 2 INCHES AWAY FROM THE BODY.

THIS LAYER IS LINKED TO OUR BASE CHAKRA. IT REFLECTS THE WELL-BEING AND HEALTH OF A PERSON.

2 THE EMOTIONAL LAYER

2 - 3 INCHES

5 - 8 CENTIMETRES

THE EMOTIONAL LAYER IS THE SECOND LAYER IN THE AURA. THIS IS LINKED TO THE SACRAL CHAKRA AND SHOWS WHERE SOMEONE IS EMOTIONALLY. IT ALSO SHOWS HOW THEY ARE FEELING AND WHAT THEY HAVE FELT EMOTIONALLY IN THE PAST.

THE EMOTIONAL LAYER IS OFTEN SHOWN IN RAINBOW COLOURS THAT CAN SHIFT AND CHANGE COLOUR, DEPENDING ON WHAT IS HAPPENING TO THE PERSON EMOTIONALLY.

3 THE MENTAL LAYER

THE MENTAL LAYER IS THE THIRD LAYER OF THE AURA. IT IS CONNECTED TO THE SOLAR PLEXUS COLOURED YELLOW AND LOCATED ABOUT 3 TO 8 INCHES AWAY FROM THE BODY.

3 - 8 INCHES

← — — — —

8 - 13 CENTIMETRES

OUR THOUGHTS FORM AND SHAPE THE MENTAL LAYER OF THE AURA.

4 THE ASTRAL LAYER

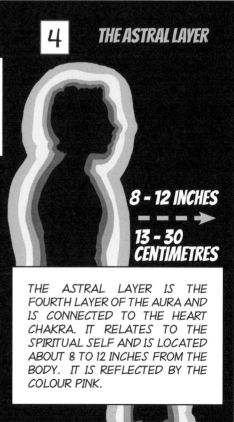

8 - 12 INCHES

— — — — →

13 - 30 CENTIMETRES

THE ASTRAL LAYER IS THE FOURTH LAYER OF THE AURA AND IS CONNECTED TO THE HEART CHAKRA. IT RELATES TO THE SPIRITUAL SELF AND IS LOCATED ABOUT 8 TO 12 INCHES FROM THE BODY. IT IS REFLECTED BY THE COLOUR PINK.

5 THE SPIRITUAL LAYER

THE SPIRITUAL LAYER IS THE FIFTH LAYER OF THE AURA AND IS LINKED TO THE THROAT CHAKRA.

THE SPIRITUAL LAYER IS FOUND ABOUT 2 FEET AWAY FROM THE BODY.

IT IS LINKED TO THE COLOUR BLUE AND RELATES TO COMMUNICATION AND CREATIVE EXPRESSION.

IT REFLECTS A PERSON'S HIGHER CONSCIOUSNESS.

2 FEET
60 CENTIMETERS

6 THE CELESTIAL LAYER

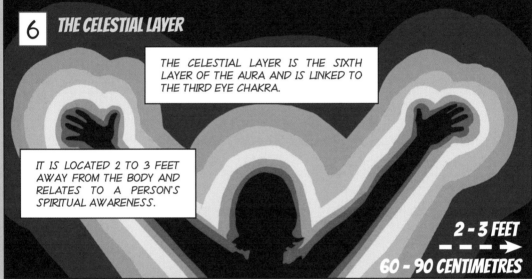

THE CELESTIAL LAYER IS THE SIXTH LAYER OF THE AURA AND IS LINKED TO THE THIRD EYE CHAKRA.

IT IS LOCATED 2 TO 3 FEET AWAY FROM THE BODY AND RELATES TO A PERSON'S SPIRITUAL AWARENESS.

2 - 3 FEET
60 - 90 CENTIMETRES

7 THE CAUSAL LAYER

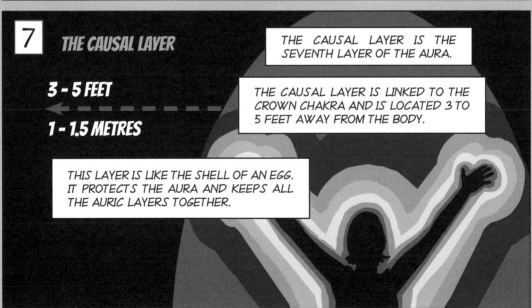

THE CAUSAL LAYER IS THE SEVENTH LAYER OF THE AURA.

THE CAUSAL LAYER IS LINKED TO THE CROWN CHAKRA AND IS LOCATED 3 TO 5 FEET AWAY FROM THE BODY.

3 - 5 FEET
1 - 1.5 METRES

THIS LAYER IS LIKE THE SHELL OF AN EGG. IT PROTECTS THE AURA AND KEEPS ALL THE AURIC LAYERS TOGETHER.

KEEPING YOUR AURA CLEAR

IT IS IMPORTANT TO LOOK AFTER YOUR ENERGY AND KEEP IT CLEAR.

A QUICK WAY TO DO THIS IS TO WORK WITH A CRYSTAL CALLED LABRADORITE

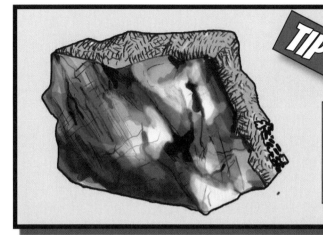

TIP

REMEMBER TO CLEAR YOUR AURA AT REGULAR TIMES.

LABRADORITE IS A CRYSTAL THAT CAN CLEANSE AND CLEAR THE AURA. IT HAS EVEN BEEN SHOWN IN KIRLIAN PHOTOGRAPHY TO HEAL TEARS AND STOP LEAKS IN THE AURA.

CLEARING THE AURA WITH LABRADORITE

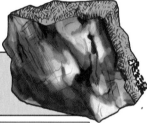

1 GET YOURSELF A PIECE OF LABRADORITE.

2 FIND YOURSELF A QUIET SPACE TO SIT OR LIE DOWN.

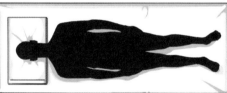

3 TURN YOUR FOCUS ONTO THE BREATH. VISUALIZE BREATHING IN A SENSE OF STILLNESS AND CALM. AS YOU EXHALE, VISUALIZE BREATHING OUT ANY TENSIONS AND STRESSES.

BREATHE IN   **BREATHE OUT**

4 HOLD YOUR PIECE OF LABRADORITE IN YOUR HANDS FOR 20 MINUTES. GENTLY CONNECT TO THE ENERGY AND THE VIBRATION OF THE CRYSTAL.

BY HOLDING THE CRYSTAL FOR THIS TIME, YOU WILL ALLOW THE CRYSTAL'S VIBRATION TO WORK WITH YOUR ENERGY. IT WILL HEAL ANY BLOCKS OR TEARS IN THE AURA.

CREATING SACRED SPACE

WHEN IT COMES TO DOING ANY PSYCHIC WORK IT IS IMPORTANT THAT WE CREATE THE RIGHT ENERGETIC SPACE TO WORK IN

AS A STARTING POINT, WORKING IN A CLUTTERED SPACE WILL NOT BE GOOD FOR YOU.

IT IS IMPORTANT TO SET ASIDE A CLEAN AND CLUTTER-FREE SPACE TO WORK IN.

BUT IT'S NOT JUST THE PHYSICAL CLUTTER WE NEED TO ATTEND TO.

WE ALSO NEED TO CONSIDER THE ENERGY THAT IS IN OUR WORK SPACE.

OUR SPACE CAN BE A BREEDING GROUND FOR NEGATIVE EMOTIONAL ENERGIES.........

....FROM PREVIOUS OWNERS,

FROM OURSELVES,

AND OUR FAMILIES AND FRIENDS.

IT IS IMPORTANT THAT WE CLEAR THIS BEFORE WE START WORKING.

EVERYTHING IS ENERGY

AS WE RESIDE IN OUR SPACE, A BUILD-UP OF ENERGY OCCURS.

DEPENDING ON THE WAY WE CHOOSE TO LIVE OUR LIVES, WE CAN CREATE DIFFERENT ENERGIES.

DAILY LIFE CAN BE STRESSFUL AT TIMES,

WE HAVE TO WORK,

PAY BILLS,

WE HAVE TO DEAL WITH EMOTIONS THAT COME UP FOR US,

COPE WITH OCCASIONAL ILLNESSES, AND DEAL WITH ENERGIES COMING IN FROM GUESTS, WHICH CAN BE POSITIVE OR NEGATIVE.

AND SOMETIMES HANDLE DIFFICULT RELATIONSHIPS.

KEEPING A CLEAR ENERGETIC SPACE TAKES SOME TIME AND DEDICATION

IT IS SOMETHING THAT YOU HAVE TO WORK AT IN ORDER TO MAINTAIN THE SPACE YOU WANT.

YOU DO THIS BY....

RAISING THE VIBRATION IN YOUR SPACE

AND BY DOING THINGS THAT CREATE HIGH VIBRATIONS,

LIKE MEDITATION

LISTENING TO HIGH VIBRATIONAL MUSIC

AND CHOOSING TO STAY POSITIVE IN YOUR THINKING AND MIND SET.

CAT MAT

CREATING SACRED SPACE

WE CAN DO A NUMBER OF THINGS TO CLEAR OUR SPACE ENERGETICALLY AND TO CREATE A SACRED SPACE TO WORK IN

SMUDGING

SMUDGING HAS BEEN USED FOR YEARS BY NATIVE AMERICANS. IT IS A POWERFUL CLEANSING TECHNIQUE, USED TO CLEAR A PERSON AND/OR A SPACE OF ANY NEGATIVE ENERGIES.

SMUDGING INVOLVES THE USE OF HERBS, MAINLY SAGE, WHICH IS EASY TO BUY IN SMALL BUNDLES.

TO SMUDGE A SPACE

1 TAKE YOUR SMUDGE STICK AND LIGHT IT WITH A CANDLE.

THEN BLOW OUT THE FLAME

ALLOWING THE SMUDGE STICK TO SMOULDER.

2 YOU MAY WANT TO STATE AN INTENTION AT THIS POINT

MY INTENTION IS TO CLEAR MY SPACE OF ANY NEGATIVE UNWANTED ENERGY IN PREPARATION FOR MY PSYCHIC AND SPIRITUAL WORK.

INTENTION IS VERY POWERFUL

BY STATING OUR INTENTION WE EMPOWER THE RITUAL OF SMUDGING AND ENFORCE WHAT IT IS THAT WE PLAN TO DO.

3 TAKING YOUR SMUDGE STICK, BEGIN TO WALK AROUND THE PERIMETER OF YOUR ROOM.

FOCUS YOUR ATTENTION ON THE CORNERS OF THE ROOM.

AS YOU CONTINUE TO SMUDGE THE ROOM, KEEP IN MIND YOUR INTENTION OF REMOVING ANY NEGATIVE ENERGY FROM THE SPACE.

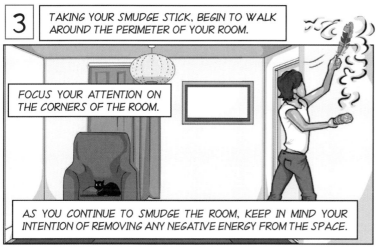

4 EITHER USE YOUR HAND, A FEATHER, OR FAN, TO MOVE THE SMOKE FROM THE SMUDGE STICK INTO THE ROOM.

5 AFTER MOVING THROUGH THE ROOM WITH YOUR SMUDGE STICK, OPEN ANY WINDOWS AND ALLOW THE SMOKE TO CLEAR.

OPENING THE WINDOWS ALLOWS UNWANTED ENERGY TO BE CLEARED FROM THE SPACE.

IT IS A GOOD IDEA TO TRY TO CLEANSE THE SPACE ON A WEEKLY BASIS.

YOU MAY ALSO WANT TO EXPAND THIS PRACTICE BEYOND YOUR WORKING SPACE.

IF YOU ARE WORKING WITH OTHERS IN THEIR SPACE DOING READINGS, OR YOU ARE AN ENERGY HEALER, IT WOULD BE ADVISABLE TO DO THIS MORE OFTEN. ENERGIES FROM THIS TYPE OF WORK CAN EASILY BUILD UP, THEREFORE IT IS IMPORTANT TO KEEP CLEARING THE SPACE.

CLEAR YOUR WHOLE HOUSE EVERY SO OFTEN, TO MAINTAIN A CLEAN AND CLEAR LIVING SPACE.

CLEAN!

SOUND CLEARING

YOU MAY ALSO WISH TO CLEAR YOUR HOUSE USING SOUND. THIS CAN BE A VERY EFFECTIVE PRACTICE TO CLEAR SPACE.

YOU COULD USE

A DRUM, A TIBETAN SINGING BOWL, CHIMES, A RATTLE OR CLAPPING WITH YOUR HANDS.

TO CLEAR YOUR SPACE WITH SOUND

TO CLEAR YOUR SPACE OF ANY NEGATIVE ENERGIES,

EITHER WITH YOUR HANDS,

OR THROUGH YOUR CHOSEN INSTRUMENT,

BEGIN TO CIRCLE THE ROOM MAKING THE SOUND.

FOCUS ON THE CORNERS, WHERE ENERGY BUILDS.

AFTER MOVING THROUGH YOUR ROOM WITH YOUR SOUND, OPEN ANY WINDOWS ALLOWING ENERGY TO BE RELEASED AND CLEARED THROUGH THE SPACE.

THE SOUND BREAKS UP THE STAGNANT ENERGY, ALLOWING IT TO BE CLEARED.

OTHER SPACE-CLEARING TECHNIQUES

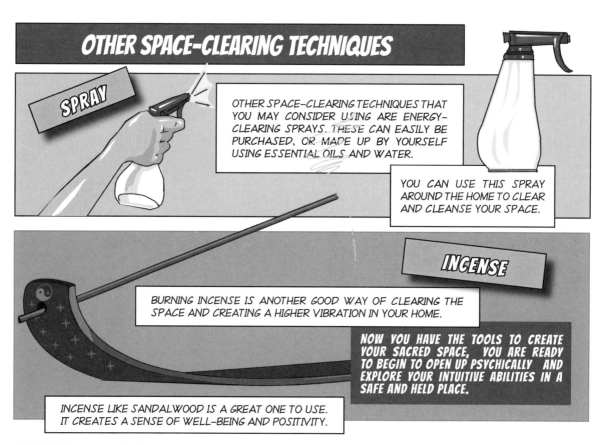

SPRAY

OTHER SPACE-CLEARING TECHNIQUES THAT YOU MAY CONSIDER USING ARE ENERGY-CLEARING SPRAYS. THESE CAN EASILY BE PURCHASED, OR MADE UP BY YOURSELF USING ESSENTIAL OILS AND WATER.

YOU CAN USE THIS SPRAY AROUND THE HOME TO CLEAR AND CLEANSE YOUR SPACE.

INCENSE

BURNING INCENSE IS ANOTHER GOOD WAY OF CLEARING THE SPACE AND CREATING A HIGHER VIBRATION IN YOUR HOME.

NOW YOU HAVE THE TOOLS TO CREATE YOUR SACRED SPACE, YOU ARE READY TO BEGIN TO OPEN UP PSYCHICALLY AND EXPLORE YOUR INTUITIVE ABILITIES IN A SAFE AND HELD PLACE.

INCENSE LIKE SANDALWOOD IS A GREAT ONE TO USE. IT CREATES A SENSE OF WELL-BEING AND POSITIVITY.

OPENING UP

OPEN   CLOSED

Chicago Bears 33
San Diego Chargers 28

♪♪ hunka hunka ♪♪
burnin' love

This is the BBC
World Service

Boil for 20mins

WHEN BEGINNING ANY INTUITIVE OR PSYCHIC DEVELOPMENT WORK, IT IS IMPORTANT TO OPEN OURSELVES UP ENERGETICALLY.

IN MANY WAYS THIS CAN BE LIKENED TO FINE-TUNING A RADIO.

OPENING UP IS A PROCESS.

BY OPENING UP OUR ENERGY CENTRES, (CHAKRAS) WE ALLOW OURSELVES TO BECOME MORE RECEPTIVE TO OUR HIGHER SELVES AND THE INFORMATION AROUND US.

IMAGINE YOURSELF AS A RADIO RECEIVER. AS YOU OPEN UP, YOU ARE SUBTLY TUNING YOUR RADIO TO PICK UP DIFFERENT TYPES OF INFORMATION.

IN ORDER TO GAIN MORE INFORMATION AND UNDERSTANDING IN THE AREA YOU ARE LOOKING INTO PSYCHICALLY, IT IS A GOOD IDEA TO OPEN AND CLOSE DOWN AT SET TIMES.

IF YOU DON'T CLOSE DOWN YOU BECOME LIKE A SPONGE AND WILL BE TOO OPEN!

THEN YOU CONTINUE TO ABSORB THE ENERGIES OF THE PEOPLE AND ENVIRONMENT AROUND YOU.

THIS CAN LEAD TO PSYCHIC BURNOUT AND EXHAUSTION. IT CAN ALSO AFFECT HOW YOU WILL BE ABLE TO WORK IN THE FUTURE.

IT'S NOT A GOOD IDEA TO STAY OPEN ALL OF THE TIME!

BY HAVING A GOOD PRACTICE (CLOSING DOWN AFTER YOU OPEN UP), YOU SAFEGUARD YOUR ENERGY AND YOU CAN LIVE YOUR LIFE WITHOUT BEING OPEN TO ABSORBING THE WORLD'S POSITIVE AND NEGATIVE EMOTIONS AND VIBRATIONS.

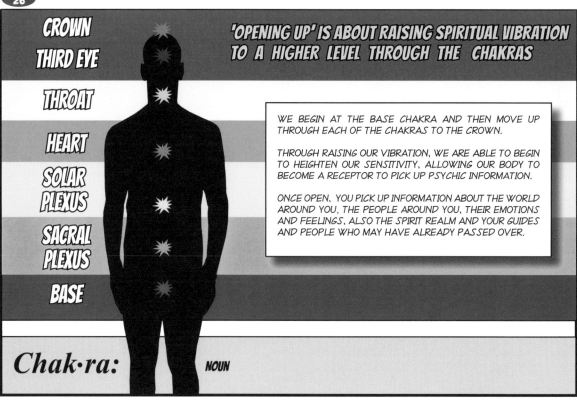

CROWN
THIRD EYE
THROAT
HEART
SOLAR PLEXUS
SACRAL PLEXUS
BASE

'OPENING UP' IS ABOUT RAISING SPIRITUAL VIBRATION TO A HIGHER LEVEL THROUGH THE CHAKRAS

WE BEGIN AT THE BASE CHAKRA AND THEN MOVE UP THROUGH EACH OF THE CHAKRAS TO THE CROWN.

THROUGH RAISING OUR VIBRATION, WE ARE ABLE TO BEGIN TO HEIGHTEN OUR SENSITIVITY, ALLOWING OUR BODY TO BECOME A RECEPTOR TO PICK UP PSYCHIC INFORMATION.

ONCE OPEN, YOU PICK UP INFORMATION ABOUT THE WORLD AROUND YOU, THE PEOPLE AROUND YOU, THEIR EMOTIONS AND FEELINGS, ALSO THE SPIRIT REALM AND YOUR GUIDES AND PEOPLE WHO MAY HAVE ALREADY PASSED OVER.

Chak·ra: NOUN

 **EXERCISE**

 **OPENING UP**

1. FIND A QUIET SPACE WHERE YOU WILL NOT BE DISTURBED.

2. SIT DOWN OR LIE DOWN AND CLOSE YOUR EYES. BEGIN TO FOCUS YOUR ATTENTION ON YOUR BREATH.

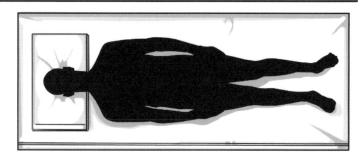

3. **INHALE** AS YOU BEGIN TO BREATHE IN, IMAGINE BREATHING IN A WHITE LIGHT THAT BRINGS CALMNESS TO THE BODY AND MIND. FEEL THIS CALMNESS WASH THROUGH THE BODY WITH THE IN-BREATH.

4. **EXHALE**

AS YOU EXHALE BEGIN TO RELEASE ANY TENSIONS, WORRIES AND ANXIETIES FROM THE DAY. VISUALIZE THEM LEAVING THE BODY ON THE OUT-BREATH.

5 | TURN YOUR FOCUS ONTO THE BASE CHAKRA LOCATED IN THE PELVIS

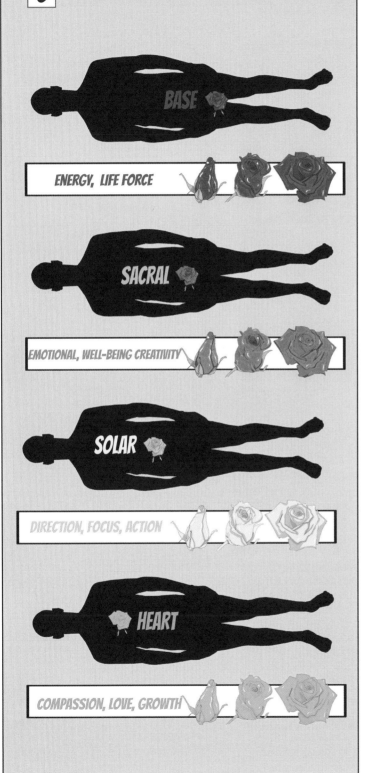

ENERGY, LIFE FORCE

SACRAL

EMOTIONAL, WELL-BEING CREATIVITY

SOLAR

DIRECTION, FOCUS, ACTION

HEART

COMPASSION, LOVE, GROWTH

VISUALIZE A BEAUTIFUL RED FLOWER THAT IS GENTLY IN BUD, RESTING ON THE TOP OF YOUR BASE CHAKRA. AS YOU BEGIN TO LINK IN WITH YOUR BASE CHAKRA, VISUALIZE THIS RED FLOWER SLOWLY BEGINNING TO OPEN INTO FULL BLOOM.

ONCE THE FLOWER IS OPEN, BEGIN TO DRAW ENERGY IN THROUGH THIS OPEN FLOWER. FEEL AND SEE THE BASE CHAKRA BEGINNING TO CHARGE WITH THIS ENERGY.

MOVE YOUR FOCUS UP TO YOUR SACRAL CHAKRA, THE CHAKRA LOCATED JUST BELOW THE NAVEL AREA. THIS TIME VISUALIZE AN ORANGE FLOWER THAT IS GENTLY IN BUD RESTING ON YOUR SACRAL CHAKRA. VISUALIZE THIS ORANGE FLOWER GENTLY OPENING INTO FULL BLOOM.

ONCE THE FLOWER IS OPEN, AGAIN BEGIN TO DRAW ENERGY IN THROUGH THIS FLOWER. SEE AND FEEL THIS ENERGY BEGINNING TO CHARGE THE SACRAL CHAKRA.

RAISE YOUR AWARENESS TO THE SOLAR PLEXUS. THE CHAKRA LOCATED BETWEEN THE TOP OF THE RIBS. VISUALIZE A YELLOW FLOWER RESTING GENTLY IN BUD ON THE SOLAR PLEXUS.

VISUALIZE AND FEEL THE FLOWER OPEN. BEGIN TO DRAW THE ENERGY INTO YOUR SOLAR PLEXUS. FEEL THIS CHAKRA BEGIN TO CHARGE WITH THE ENERGY THAT YOU ARE DRAWING IN.

CONTINUE UPWARDS TO THE HEART CHAKRA. VISUALIZE A GREEN FLOWER IN BUD RESTING ON THE HEART CHAKRA. IMAGINE OPENING UP THIS FLOWER AND DRAWING ENERGY INTO THE HEART CHAKRA.

AS YOU DO THIS BECOME AWARE OF THE CHAKRA'S VIBRATION RISING AND EMPOWERING ITSELF.

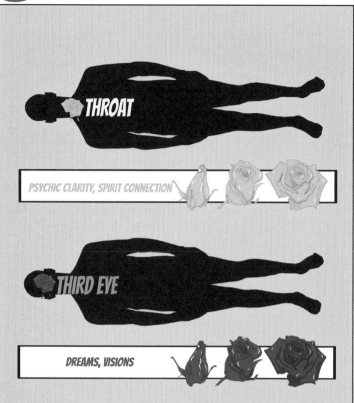

NOW SHIFT YOUR FOCUS TO THE THROAT CHAKRA. VISUALIZE A BEAUTIFUL BLUE FLOWER IN BUD RESTING ON YOUR THROAT CHAKRA. SLOWLY BEGIN TO OPEN THE PETALS UNTIL THE FLOWER OPENS.

AS IT OPENS, BEGIN TO VISUALIZE DRAWING ENERGY INTO THE THROAT CHAKRA. FEEL YOUR VIBRATION BEGIN TO RISE AS YOU CONTINUE TO DRAW ENERGY INTO EACH OF THE CHAKRAS.

FROM THE THROAT CHAKRA, WE MOVE OUR ATTENTION UP TO OUR THIRD EYE. THIS IS THE CHAKRA THAT IS RESPONSIBLE FOR OUR CLAIRVOYANCE AND OUR ABILITY TO SEE THINGS INTUITIVELY.

HERE YOU WILL SEE A DARK BLUE OR PURPLE FLOWER IN BUD. VISUALIZE OPENING THIS FLOWER, AND WHEN THE FLOWER IS OPEN, DRAW ENERGY INTO THE FLOWER.

THROAT

PSYCHIC CLARITY, SPIRIT CONNECTION

THIRD EYE

DREAMS, VISIONS

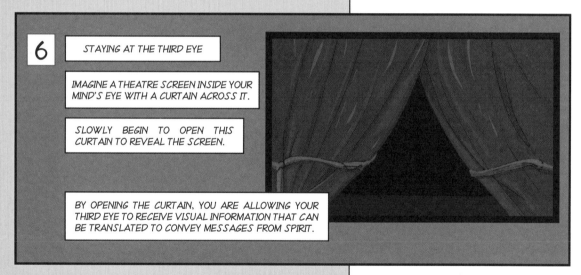

6

STAYING AT THE THIRD EYE

IMAGINE A THEATRE SCREEN INSIDE YOUR MIND'S EYE WITH A CURTAIN ACROSS IT.

SLOWLY BEGIN TO OPEN THIS CURTAIN TO REVEAL THE SCREEN.

BY OPENING THE CURTAIN, YOU ARE ALLOWING YOUR THIRD EYE TO RECEIVE VISUAL INFORMATION THAT CAN BE TRANSLATED TO CONVEY MESSAGES FROM SPIRIT.

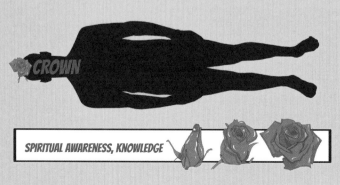

CROWN

SPIRITUAL AWARENESS, KNOWLEDGE

LEAVING THE THIRD EYE, JOURNEY UP FURTHER TO THE CROWN CHAKRA, WHICH IS LOCATED ON THE TOP OF THE HEAD. ONCE HERE, VISUALIZE A WHITE OR PURPLE FLOWER IN BUD. GENTLY OPEN THE FLOWER.

ONCE IT IS OPEN, BEGIN TO DRAW ENERGY INTO THE CROWN CHAKRA. FEEL THE ENERGY RISING.

OPENING UP

7 YOU HAVE OPENED ALL YOUR CHAKRAS, SO BEGIN TO FEEL INTO THE ENERGY AND THE NEW VIBRATIONS THAT CAN ARISE FROM THESE CHAKRAS BEING OPEN.

YOU ARE NOW DRAWING IN UNIVERSAL ENERGY TO CHARGE THESE CHAKRAS AND RAISE YOUR VIBRATION.

WHAT ARE THEY?

OFTEN WHEN WE OPEN UP, WE FEEL MORE SENSITIVE. THIS MAY MAKE US FEEL MORE TINGLY.

YOU MAY FIND THAT SOUND IS LOUDER AND THINGS ARE BRIGHTER. THIS IS BECAUSE YOU ARE IN A MORE RECEPTIVE STATE.

8 MAKE A NOTE OF THESE FEELINGS AND SENSATIONS.

PROTECTION

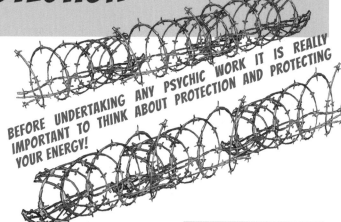

BEFORE UNDERTAKING ANY PSYCHIC WORK IT IS REALLY IMPORTANT TO THINK ABOUT PROTECTION AND PROTECTING YOUR ENERGY!

AFTER OPENING UP, YOU ARE SENSITIVE TO YOUR ENERGY PICKING UP PSYCHIC INFORMATION.

WHILE THE MAJORITY OF THIS ENERGY WILL BE POSITIVE, THERE COULD BE AN ELEMENT THAT MAY NOT BE.

YOU ARE OPEN TO PICKING UP THE ENERGY OF PEOPLE, PLACES AND SPIRIT, ALL AROUND YOU.

Bad mood

WITHOUT PROTECTION, YOU MAY FIND YOURSELF ABSORBING UNWANTED NEGATIVE ENERGY.

PROTECTION

PROTECTION IS A TECHNIQUE THAT PSYCHICS AND ENERGY WORKERS USE TO PROTECT THEMSELVES.

PROTECTION CAN OFTEN BE OVERLOOKED BY PEOPLE WORKING PSYCHICALLY.

PSYCHIC BURNOUT

PSYCHIC BURNOUT IS SOMETHING THAT OCCURS WHEN A PSYCHIC OR HIGHLY INTUITIVE PERSON ABSORBS A LOT OF NEGATIVE ENERGY FROM THEIR ENVIRONMENT.

THIS MAY LEAVE THEM FEELING DRAINED, TIRED, AND UNABLE TO WORK QUITE AS EFFECTIVELY.

CAN'T MOVE! TOO EXHAUSTED...... EVEN TO USE THE REMOTE!

REMEMBER

AS A HIGHLY SENSITIVE PERSON, YOU ARE VERY OPEN TO THE ENERGIES AND ATMOSPHERES AROUND YOU. YOU MAY ABSORB THESE EMOTIONS INTO YOUR AURA, WHERE THEY COULD GET LODGED.

YOU MIGHT THEN FIND YOURSELF FEELING TIRED AND DRAINED BY THIS AND NOT AS ENERGETIC OR TUNED IN AS BEFORE.

WHAT PSYCHIC PROTECTION DOES IS CREATE A BARRIER BETWEEN YOU AND THE ENERGIES AT WORK AROUND YOU,

ALLOWING YOU TO SENSE THE ENERGIES WITHOUT ABSORBING THEM.

THERE ARE A NUMBER OF TECHNIQUES THAT WE CAN USE FOR PSYCHIC PROTECTION.

SOME PEOPLE PREFER VISUALIZATIONS, WHILE A LESS VISUAL PERSON MAY PREFER TO USE OTHER TECHNIQUES: CRYSTALS, SMUDGING OR SOUND ENERGY, SUCH AS CLAPPING.

VISUALISATIONS

OTHER TECHNIQUES

IN THIS CHAPTER WE WILL EXPLORE A FEW TECHNIQUES YOU CAN USE TO PROTECT YOURSELF. AFTER TRYING EACH OF THEM, SEE WHICH ONE WORKS FOR YOU INTUITIVELY, AND ADOPT THAT SPECIFIC TECHNIQUE TO APPLY YOUR PSYCHIC PROTECTION.

EXERCISE

PROTECTIVE BUBBLE

TO APPLY THE PROTECTIVE BUBBLE

1 FIND YOURSELF A SPACE THAT IS QUIET, WHERE YOU WILL NOT BE DISTURBED OR HAVE ANY DISTRACTIONS. SIT OR LIE DOWN. MAKE YOURSELF COMFORTABLE AND RELAXED.

THE PROTECTIVE BUBBLE IS A SIMPLE VISUALIZATION TECHNIQUE THAT YOU CAN USE TO PROTECT YOURSELF. IT IS VERY SIMPLE, QUICK AND EFFECTIVE.

2 FOCUS YOUR ATTENTION AWAY FROM YOUR THOUGHTS

3 AND ONTO YOUR BREATH. VISUALIZE BREATHING IN A SENSE OF CALMNESS AND PEACE WITH THE IN-BREATH.

4 USE THE OUT-BREATH TO LET GO OF ANY TENSIONS OR STRESSES. EXPEL THEM AS YOU EXHALE.

5 IMAGINE A GIANT BUBBLE AROUND YOU.

6 SENSE THIS BUBBLE FORMING, GROWING AND MAINTAINING A FIXED SHAPE.

7 VISUALIZE GROWING A SHELL ALL AROUND THE OUTSIDE OF THIS BUBBLE.

8
SEE THIS SHELL EXPANDING TO FORM A PROTECTIVE LAYER A COUPLE OF INCHES THICK.
BEGIN TO FILL THE SPACE BETWEEN YOU AND THE SHELL OF THIS BUBBLE WITH A BEAUTIFUL WHITE PROTECTIVE LIGHT.
SENSE THIS WHITE LIGHT ENCIRCLING AND SURROUNDING YOU, CREATING A PROTECTIVE ENERGY.

9
TURN YOUR ATTENTION TO THE OUTSIDE OF THE BUBBLE. IMAGINE PLACING MIRRORS THAT FACE OUTWARDS ALL AROUND ITS SURFACE.
GRRRR
THE OUTSIDE OF YOUR BUBBLE BECOMES A REFLECTIVE MIRRORED SURFACE. THESE MIRRORS ARE IN PLACE TO REFLECT OFF ANY NEGATIVE ENERGY AROUND YOU.
YOU HAVE NOW SUCCESSFULLY CREATED YOUR OWN PROTECTIVE BUBBLE. YOU CAN NOW DO ANY PSYCHIC WORK IN A SPACE WHERE YOU ARE PROTECTED.

FOR THOSE PEOPLE WHO FIND IT HARD TO VISUALIZE

YOU MAY PREFER ANOTHER TECHNIQUE CALLED
'THE PROTECTIVE CLOAK OR ARMOUR'.

EXERCISE — **CLOAK OR ARMOUR:**

1 WITH THE PROTECTIVE CLOAK OR ARMOUR TECHNIQUE, BEGIN IN A QUIET PLACE WHERE YOU WILL NOT BE DISTURBED.

FOCUS YOUR ATTENTION ONTO YOUR BREATH.

VISUALIZE BREATHING IN A SENSE OF CALMNESS AND PEACE WITH THE IN-BREATH.

EXPEL ANY NEGATIVE THOUGHTS AS YOU EXHALE.

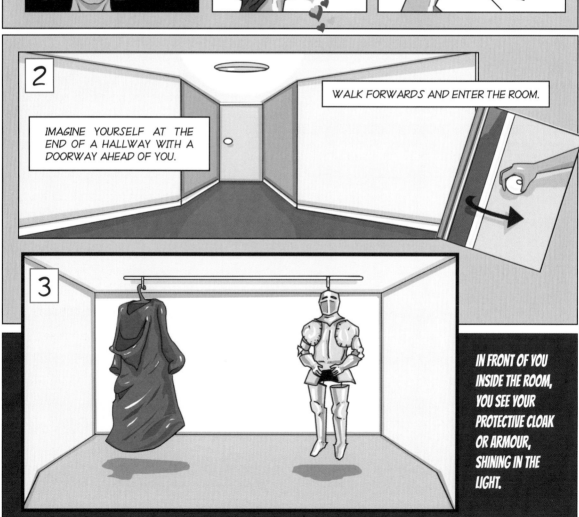

2 IMAGINE YOURSELF AT THE END OF A HALLWAY WITH A DOORWAY AHEAD OF YOU.

WALK FORWARDS AND ENTER THE ROOM.

3 IN FRONT OF YOU INSIDE THE ROOM, YOU SEE YOUR PROTECTIVE CLOAK OR ARMOUR, SHINING IN THE LIGHT.

APPROACH YOUR CLOAK OR ARMOUR

SLOWLY BEGIN TO PUT YOUR CLOAK OR ARMOUR ONTO YOUR BODY.

FOR THOSE OF YOU WHO ARE NOT VISUAL

PRETEND TO PUT ON THE CLOAK OR ARMOUR AND FEEL IT ALL AROUND YOU. FASTEN IT UP SO IT CONCEALS YOU.

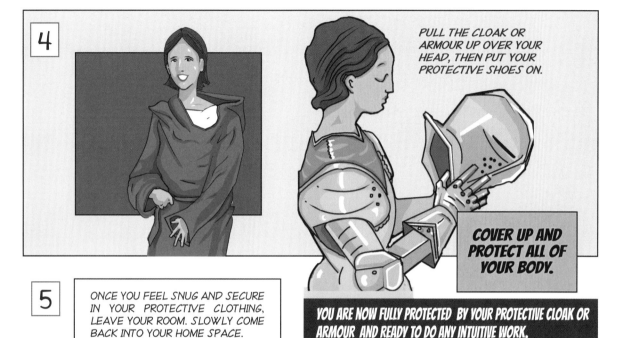

4

PULL THE CLOAK OR ARMOUR UP OVER YOUR HEAD, THEN PUT YOUR PROTECTIVE SHOES ON.

COVER UP AND PROTECT ALL OF YOUR BODY.

5 ONCE YOU FEEL SNUG AND SECURE IN YOUR PROTECTIVE CLOTHING, LEAVE YOUR ROOM. SLOWLY COME BACK INTO YOUR HOME SPACE.

YOU ARE NOW FULLY PROTECTED BY YOUR PROTECTIVE CLOAK OR ARMOUR AND READY TO DO ANY INTUITIVE WORK.

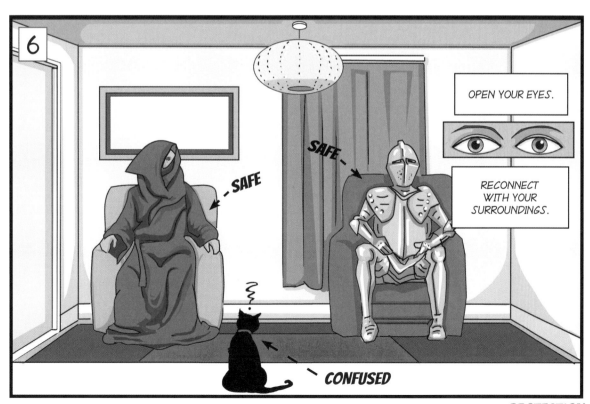

6

OPEN YOUR EYES.

RECONNECT WITH YOUR SURROUNDINGS.

- SAFE

SAFE - -

CONFUSED

PROTECTION

YOUR PROTECTIVE CLOAK

NOW THAT YOU HAVE COMPLETED YOUR VISUALIZATION TO FIND YOUR PROTECTIVE CLOAK OR ARMOUR, IT IS TIME TO MAKE A RECORD OF WHAT YOU HAVE FOUND.

FILING

KEEPING A RECORD OF WHAT YOU HAVE LEARNT WILL HELP YOU BUILD A TOOLBOX OF KNOWLEDGE.

ALL OF THIS INFORMATION HELPS TO BUILD YOUR SKILL BASE AND DEEPEN YOUR INTUITIVE UNDERSTANDING OF HOW YOU WORK AND COMMUNICATE.

FOR THIS EXERCISE YOU WILL NEED:

A YOUR PROTECTIVE CLOAK TEMPLATE WORKSHEET (SEE PAGE 40).

B SOME COLOUR PENCILs

D A BLACK OR BLUE PEN

C PASTELS

IN ORDER TO DO THIS EXERCISE YOU WILL HAVE DONE THE VISUALIZATION TO FIND YOUR PROTECTIVE CLOAK.

YOU MAY HAVE DONE THIS IN THE PREVIOUS CHAPTER OR LISTENED TO THE GUIDED VISUALIZATION ON THE **OPENING2INTUITION** CD.

TRACK 4

OPENING **2**intuition STARTER AUDIO-CD

KAREN GRACE *comic* LUCY BYATT *illustration* KIM ROBERTS *text*

FIND A QUIET SPACE WHERE YOU HAVE A TABLE AND PLENTY OF ROOM TO WORK IN.

TAKE YOUR PROTECTIVE CLOAK TEMPLATE WORKSHEET. YOU WILL SEE THAT YOU HAVE A SILHOUETTE OF A PERSON ON YOUR WORKSHEET.

THIS ACTS AS A GUIDE FOR YOU TO DRAW YOUR PROTECTIVE CLOAK OR ARMOUR.

DON'T WORRY ABOUT YOUR ARTISTIC SKILLS

WHAT YOU ARE DOING HERE IS DRAWING AND CAPTURING THE IMAGE OF YOUR PROTECTIVE CLOAK OR ARMOUR.

SPEND A MOMENT THINKING BACK ON YOUR VISUALIZATION.

THINK ABOUT YOUR JOURNEY TO THE CLOAK.

WHAT DID YOU NOTICE WHEN YOU FIRST SAW YOUR CLOAK OR ARMOUR?

WHAT COLOUR WAS IT?

WHAT TEXTURE WAS IT?

DIMPLED?

SMOOTH?

ROUGH? HARD?

RECALL ALL OF YOUR DETAILS INSIDE THE BOX ON THE WORKSHEET. USE ANOTHER CLEAR SHEET OF PAPER IF NECESSARY.

AT A LATER DATE, YOU MAY LOOK BACK ON THIS INFORMATION AND BE REMINDED OF IMPORTANT DETAILS YOU MISSED!

AFTER TAKING A MOMENT TO GATHER ALL THE INFORMATION THAT YOU CAN REMEMBER,

USE YOUR COLOUR PASTEL AND PENCILS TO DRAW YOUR PROTECTIVE CLOAK OR ARMOUR.

FEEL FREE TO ADD IN ANY INFORMATION ABOUT YOUR CLOAK IN THE SPACE SURROUNDING IT.

DO THIS EXERCISE AS MANY TIMES AS YOU FEEL YOU NEED TO... YOU CAN CHANGE YOUR CLOAK TO SUIT YOUR SITUATION.

IT'S GOOD TO MAKE NOTES, AS DETAILS CAN BE FORGOTTEN.

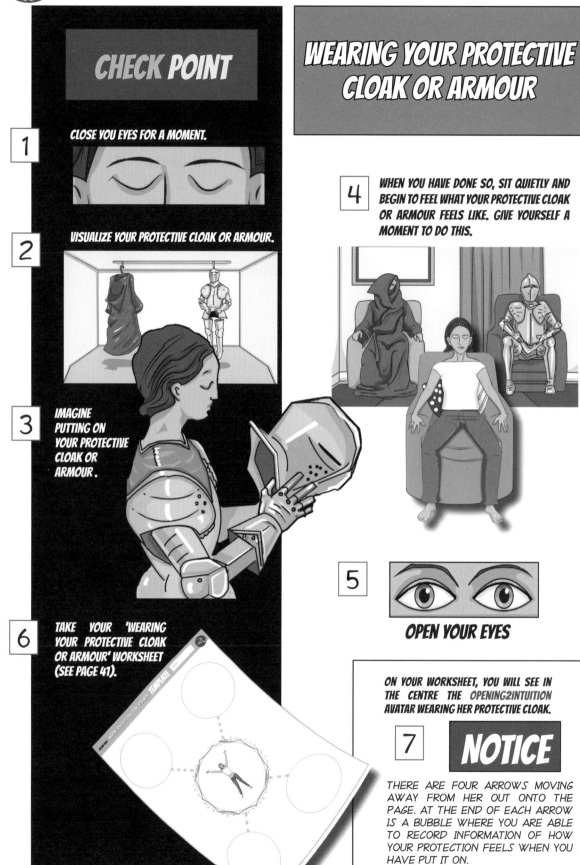

CHECK POINT

WEARING YOUR PROTECTIVE CLOAK OR ARMOUR

1 CLOSE YOU EYES FOR A MOMENT.

2 VISUALIZE YOUR PROTECTIVE CLOAK OR ARMOUR.

3 IMAGINE PUTTING ON YOUR PROTECTIVE CLOAK OR ARMOUR.

4 WHEN YOU HAVE DONE SO, SIT QUIETLY AND BEGIN TO FEEL WHAT YOUR PROTECTIVE CLOAK OR ARMOUR FEELS LIKE. GIVE YOURSELF A MOMENT TO DO THIS.

5 OPEN YOUR EYES

6 TAKE YOUR 'WEARING YOUR PROTECTIVE CLOAK OR ARMOUR' WORKSHEET (SEE PAGE 41).

ON YOUR WORKSHEET, YOU WILL SEE IN THE CENTRE THE OPENING2INTUITION AVATAR WEARING HER PROTECTIVE CLOAK.

7 **NOTICE**

THERE ARE FOUR ARROWS MOVING AWAY FROM HER OUT ONTO THE PAGE. AT THE END OF EACH ARROW IS A BUBBLE WHERE YOU ARE ABLE TO RECORD INFORMATION OF HOW YOUR PROTECTION FEELS WHEN YOU HAVE PUT IT ON.

PROTECTION

8 THINK ABOUT THE FEELINGS THAT WERE CREATED WHEN YOU PUT ON YOUR PROTECTIVE CLOAK OR ARMOUR.

DID THE PROTECTIVE CLOAK OR ARMOUR FEEL;

STRONG AND WEIGHTED?
LIGHT BUT POWERFUL?
MAGNETIC OR ELECTRICAL?

9 GO A LITTLE DEEPER AND USE YOUR IMAGINATION

HOW DO YOU FEEL YOUR PROTECTIVE CLOAK OR ARMOUR KEEPS NEGATIVE ENERGY OUT OF YOUR ENERGY FIELD?

MAYBE YOUR CLOAK HAS AN INVISIBLE ELECTRICAL FIELD THAT FRIES ANY UNWANTED ENERGY?

PERHAPS

YOUR ARMOUR HAS A VACUUM THAT SUCKS OUT ANY NEGATIVE ENERGY?

10

TAKE A MOMENT NOW TO FILL IN THE BUBBLES ON THE WORKSHEET AND RECORD HOW YOUR PROTECTIVE CLOAK OR ARMOUR MAKES YOU FEEL WHEN YOU WEAR IT.

PROTECTION

RECORD SHEET 01

DATE:

PROTECTIVE CLOAK
TEMPLATE

GO TO ganxy.com/i/111812 TO DOWNLOAD THIS TEMPLATE

NAME AND BRIEF DESCRIPTION

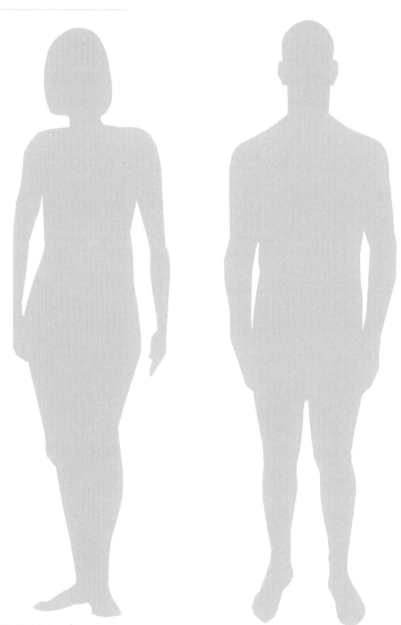

NOTES: (USE ANOTHER SHEET IF NEEDED)

FINDHORN PRESS

RECORD SHEET 02

DATE:

WEARING YOUR PROTECTIVE CLOAK
OR ARMOUR TEMPLATE

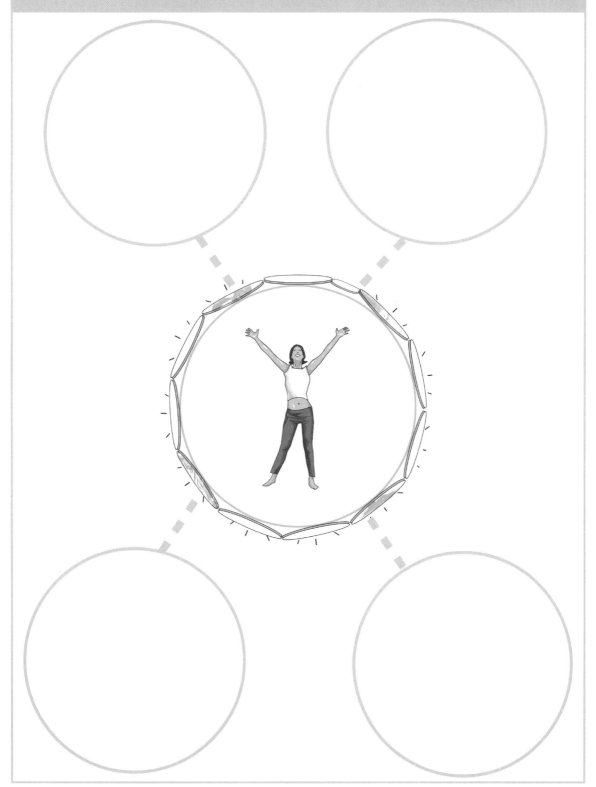

YOU CAN REINFORCE YOUR PROTECTION BY WORKING WITH SPECIFIC CRYSTALS

CRYSTALS FOR PROTECTION

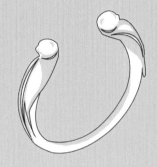

WITH CRYSTALS, YOU WORK WITH THEM BY CARRYING A SMALL PIECE ON YOUR PERSON. YOU ALLOW THEIR ENERGY TO MIX WITH YOUR AURA. YOU MIGHT WANT TO CARRY CERTAIN CRYSTALS ON YOU WHEN YOU ARE WORKING TO AID YOUR PROTECTION.

ALTERNATIVELY, YOU MAY WANT TO WEAR YOUR CRYSTAL IN A PIECE OF JEWELLERY LIKE AN AMULET OR BRACELET.

WHAT CRYSTALS CAN I USE TO PROTECT MYSELF?

THERE ARE A NUMBER OF CRYSTALS THAT YOU CAN USE FOR PROTECTION. HERE ARE A FEW YOU MAY LIKE TO CONSIDER.

SUGILITE: A PROTECTIVE STONE THAT WILL PROTECT YOUR AURA AND YOUR ENERGY.

BLACK TOURMALINE: ABSORBS NEGATIVITY, PROTECTS AGAINST PSYCHIC ATTACK AND AGAINST NEGATIVE THOUGHT-FORMS AND ENERGIES.

RUBY: SHIELDS AGAINST PSYCHIC ATTACK.

OBSIDIAN: STOPS NEGATIVE INFLUENCES AND ENERGIES FROM PENETRATING YOUR AURA AND ENERGY SYSTEM.

LABRADORITE: THIS STONE PROTECTS THE AURA FROM NEGATIVE ENERGY. IT PREVENTS PSYCHIC ATTACK AND PSYCHIC VAMPIRES FROM DRAINING YOU.

YOU MAY WANT TO EXPLORE OTHER CRYSTALS YOURSELF. WHEN DOING THIS, INTUITIVELY DECIDE WHICH CRYSTALS WORK BEST FOR YOU. USE THE ONES YOU ARE MOST DRAWN TO, AND WORK WITH THESE FOR YOUR PROTECTION.

WHEN TO USE PSYCHIC PROTECTION

IT IS BEST APPLIED WHEN YOU HAVE COMPLETED YOUR OPENING UP AND BEFORE YOU START ANY PSYCHIC WORK.

IT IS *IMPORTANT* TO USE YOUR PSYCHIC PROTECTION *WHENEVER* YOU DO ANY PSYCHIC OR INTUITIVE WORK.

HOWEVER

IF YOU ARE A NATURALLY SENSITIVE PERSON, YOU MAY FIND THAT YOU CAN EASILY ABSORB PEOPLE'S FEELINGS AND THE ENERGIES OF CERTAIN PLACES AROUND YOU.

THIS MAY AFFECT HOW YOU FEEL.

SO, FOR EXAMPLE:

YOU MIGHT BE AROUND SOMEONE AT HOME OR AT WORK WHO IS QUITE NEGATIVE. YOU MAY FIND YOURSELF FEELING DRAINED AND TIRED AS A RESULT OF BEING AROUND THEIR NEGATIVITY.

IN A CASE LIKE THIS:

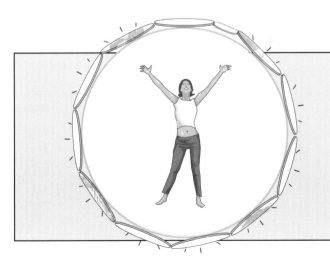

IT WOULD BE ADVISABLE TO MAKE PSYCHIC PROTECTION PART OF SOMETHING THAT YOU DO ON A DAILY BASIS. IT WOULD BE A GOOD IDEA TO START YOUR DAY BY PUTTING ON YOUR PSYCHIC PROTECTION.

PROTECTION

PART OF WORKING SAFELY WITH YOUR INTUITION AND DOING ENERGY WORK IS MAINTAINING A CLEAR ENERGY FIELD YOURSELF.

CHECKING IN WITH YOURSELF AND YOUR ENERGY

ON A DAY-TO-DAY BASIS, WE ENCOUNTER LOTS OF DIFFERENT ENERGIES!

CLEARING YOUR ENERGY

YOU MAY BE AT WORK AND YOUR COLLEAGUE IS FRUSTRATED AND UPSET ABOUT A HOME SITUATION. SHE SPENDS HER LUNCH HOUR TALKING TO YOU ABOUT IT.

I know! Then he said if she goes ahead with it he'd call the police....I said ..What about the children? *Then she said mom you've got to help!!! So I called....*

OOOH! AWFUL

WHAT HAS HAPPENED HERE IS THAT YOU HAVE PICKED UP YOUR COLLEAGUE'S NEGATIVE FEELINGS, CAUSING YOU TO FEEL TIRED AND DRAINED.

WHEN WORKING WITH ENERGY, IT IS IMPORTANT TO REGULARLY CHECK IN WITH HOW YOUR ENERGY FEELS.

BY DOING THIS, YOU CAN SEE IF YOU HAVE ANY BLOCKS IN YOUR ENERGY,

TO DO THIS, YOU CAN USE A VERY SIMPLE TECHNIQUE CALLED SCANNING. THIS INVOLVES INTUITIVELY SCANNING THROUGH YOUR BODY, CHECKING FOR ANY ENERGY BLOCKS OR DISTURBANCES.

EXERCISE — SCANNING

SCANNING YOUR ENERGY FIELD

1 BEGIN BY FINDING YOURSELF A QUIET SPACE WHERE YOU ARE FREE FROM ANY DISTRACTIONS AND WON'T BE DISTURBED.

2 TAKE A MOMENT TO GET YOURSELF COMFORTABLE. YOU CAN DO THIS EXERCISE SEATED OR LYING ON THE FLOOR, WHICHEVER ONE FEELS MOST COMFORTABLE FOR YOU.

3  **CLOSE YOUR EYES**

AND BEGIN TO FOCUS ON YOUR BREATH.

4 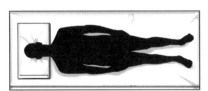 FOCUS ON BREATHING IN A SENSE OF STILLNESS WITH THE IN-BREATH.

5 AS YOU EXHALE, IMAGINE BREATHING OUT ANY SENSE OF STRESS AND TENSION,

RELEASING THIS THROUGH THE OUT-BREATH.

6

AS YOU BEGIN TO FEEL MORE RELAXED, TURN YOUR AWARENESS TO THE TOP OF YOUR HEAD. FOCUS YOUR ATTENTION THERE.

7 BEAM OF LIGHT

WHAT YOU ARE GOING TO DO NOW IS IMAGINE THAT YOU ARE MOVING AN IMAGINARY BEAM OF LIGHT DOWN THROUGH YOUR BODY. THIS BEAM OF LIGHT IS ACTING AS A PSYCHIC SCANNER, DETECTING ANY BLOCKS IN YOUR ENERGY FIELD.

8

SLOWLY MOVE THE BEAM OF LIGHT DOWN THROUGH YOUR BODY. START BY SCANNING THE TOP OF THE HEAD AND WORKING DOWN THROUGH THE FOREHEAD OVER THE EYES.

9

BEGIN TO FEEL YOUR ENERGY. LOOK OUT FOR ANY SENSATIONS THAT SUGGEST A BLOCK IN YOUR ENERGY FIELD. YOU MAY FIND THAT THE ENERGY SUDDENLY FEELS HEAVIER OR IS COLDER.

10

USE YOUR CLAIRVOYANCE. IT MAY BE THAT YOU SEE A BLOCK IN THE ENERGY. PERHAPS YOU SEE A DARKER COLOUR OR AN ENERGETIC OBJECT YOU FEEL SHOULDN'T BE THERE.

11

YOU MAY FIND THAT YOU BEGIN TO PICK UP BLOCKS IN YOUR ENERGY FIELD.

12

WORK DOWN THROUGH YOUR BODY MOVING THE SCANNER AND THE BEAM OF LIGHT THROUGH TO THE FEET.

13

ALLOW YOURSELF TO PICK UP ANY BLOCKS. MAKE A MENTAL NOTE OF WHERE THESE ARE. YOU WILL RE-SCAN AFTER DOING A CLEARING EXERCISE TO SEE IF THESE BLOCKS HAVE BEEN REMOVED.

14

ONCE YOU HAVE SCANNED THROUGH YOUR BODY, SLOWLY OPEN YOUR EYES AND COME BACK INTO THE ROOM.

YOU MAY WANT TO MAKE A NOTE OF WHERE YOU HAVE PICKED UP ANY BLOCKS, BEFORE PREPARING TO CLEAR YOUR ENERGY FIELD. WE RECOMMEND YOU USE THE BODY ENERGY MAP TEMPLATE (SEE PAGE 45).

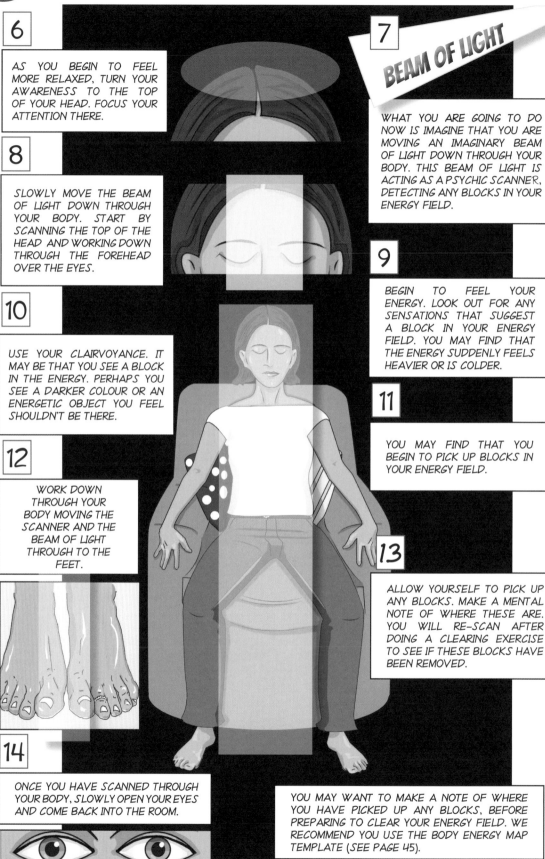

CLEARING YOUR ENERGY

THERE ARE A NUMBER OF WAYS THAT YOU CAN CLEAR YOUR ENERGY FIELD. IT IS UP TO YOU TO CHOOSE THE ONE THAT WORKS BEST FOR YOU INTUITIVELY.

SMUDGING

ONE SIMPLE AND EFFECTIVE WAY OF CLEARING YOUR ENERGY IS TO DO SOMETHING CALLED SMUDGING. SMUDGING IS A CLEARING PROCESS THAT INVOLVES THE USE OF AMERICAN SAGE.

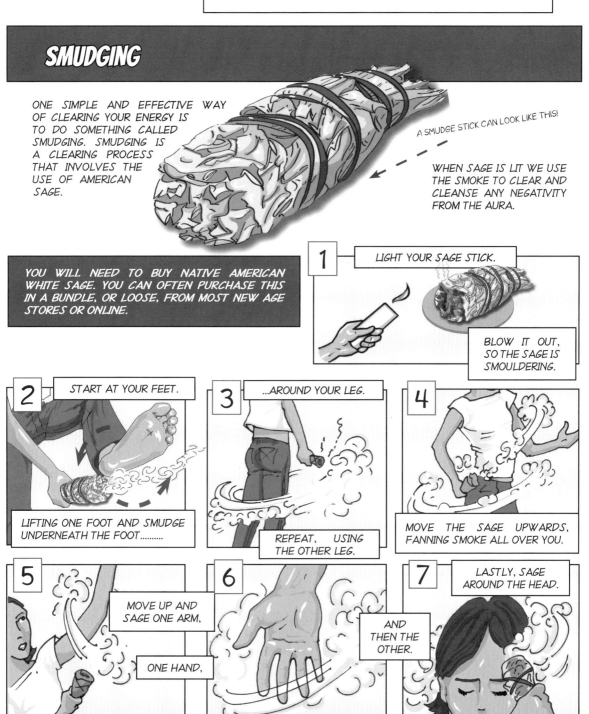

A SMUDGE STICK CAN LOOK LIKE THIS!

WHEN SAGE IS LIT WE USE THE SMOKE TO CLEAR AND CLEANSE ANY NEGATIVITY FROM THE AURA.

YOU WILL NEED TO BUY NATIVE AMERICAN WHITE SAGE. YOU CAN OFTEN PURCHASE THIS IN A BUNDLE, OR LOOSE, FROM MOST NEW AGE STORES OR ONLINE.

1 LIGHT YOUR SAGE STICK.

BLOW IT OUT, SO THE SAGE IS SMOULDERING.

2 START AT YOUR FEET.

LIFTING ONE FOOT AND SMUDGE UNDERNEATH THE FOOT.........

3 ...AROUND YOUR LEG.

REPEAT, USING THE OTHER LEG.

4 MOVE THE SAGE UPWARDS, FANNING SMOKE ALL OVER YOU.

5 MOVE UP AND SAGE ONE ARM,

ONE HAND,

6 AND THEN THE OTHER.

7 LASTLY, SAGE AROUND THE HEAD.

THIS PROCESS WILL CLEAR AND REMOVE ANY NEGATIVE AND UNWANTED ENERGY FROM THE AURA.

CLEARING YOUR ENERGY

ANOTHER WAY TO SIMPLY AND EFFECTIVELY CLEAR YOUR ENERGY IS TO USE A VISUALIZATION CALLED THE WATERFALL OF LIGHT.

THIS VISUALIZATION IS A CLEARING EXERCISE. IT WILL CLEAR YOUR ENERGY OF ANY BLOCKS AND RECHARGE YOUR ENERGETIC FIELD WITH HEALING WHITE LIGHT.

VISUALIZATION — **WATERFALL OF LIGHT** — TRACK 2

FIND A QUIET PLACE WHERE YOU WILL NOT BE DISTURBED FOR THE NEXT 10 TO 15 MINUTES.

1. SIT OR LIE DOWN AND ALLOW YOURSELF TO RELAX.

2. BREATHE IN DEEPLY. FEEL YOUR CHEST EXPANDING WITH AIR.

3. AS YOU BREATH OUT, VISUALIZE LETTING GO OF ANY STRESSES AND TENSIONS THAT YOU HAVE BEEN HOLDING ONTO.

4. GENTLY CLOSE YOUR EYES, AND BEGIN TO FOCUS ON YOUR BREATHING.

VISUALIZE THIS LEAVING YOUR BODY WITH THE OUT-BREATH.

5. AS YOU BREATHE IN, VISUALIZE BREATHING IN A NEW SENSE OF STILLNESS AND PEACE. WITH EACH BREATH.........

FEEL YOURSELF BECOMING.........

CALMNESS

CALMER AND CALMER.

6 IMAGINE THAT YOU ARE SITTING UNDERNEATH A BEAUTIFUL WATERFALL OF LIGHT..........

THIS WATERFALL OF LIGHT IS RAINING GOLDEN WHITE LIGHT DOWN ONTO YOU.

7 AS YOU SIT UNDER THE WATER, IMAGINE THE WATERFALL OF LIGHT WASHING AWAY ANY BLOCKAGES IN YOUR ENERGY. VISUALIZE WATCHING IT WASH AWAY AS IF IT IS DIRTY WATER.

8 IMAGINE OPENING A DRAIN IN THE MIDDLE OF THE FLOOR IN FRONT OF YOU. IMAGINE THE WHITE LIGHT FROM THE WATERFALL WASHING OVER YOU AND AWAY INTO THIS DRAIN.

9 SIT UNDERNEATH THIS WATERFALL OF LIGHT. ALLOW ITS ENERGY TO CONTINUE TO CHARGE YOUR ENERGY FIELD.

10 ALLOW THE WATERFALL OF LIGHT TO WASH AWAY ALL THE BLOCKAGES. CONTINUE THIS UNTIL YOU SEE THAT THE WATER FROM THE WATERFALL OF LIGHT IS RUNNING CLEAR.

11 YOU CAN SIT IN THIS POWERFUL ENERGY OF LIGHT AND ALLOW IT TO CHARGE YOUR ENERGY FOR AS LONG AS YOU NEED.

12 WHEN YOU ARE READY, SLOWLY OPEN YOUR EYES AND RETURN TO THE ROOM.

DO THE SCANNING EXERCISE AGAIN. WHEN YOU RE-SCAN YOU SHOULD FIND THAT THERE ARE NO BLOCKAGES IN YOUR ENERGY FIELD.

IT IS ADVISABLE TO DO YOUR SCANNING AND CLEARING ON A DAILY BASIS. THIS WILL ENSURE THAT YOUR ENERGY FIELD IS CLEAR.

CLEARING YOUR ENERGY

RECORD SHEET 03

DATE:

GO TO ganxy.com/i/111812 TO DOWNLOAD THIS TEMPLATE

BODY ENERGY MAP
TEMPLATE

USE COLOUR IF DESIRED. MARK WHERE YOU HAVE EXPERIENCED A BLOCKAGE. REMEMBER TO DATE YOUR LIGHT-SCANNING EXERCISE, IN ORDER TO SEE THE DEVELOPMENT AND CLEANSING, OVER A PERIOD OF TIME.

CLOSING DOWN

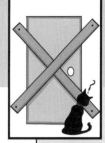

AFTER OPENING UP TO DO ANY PSYCHIC WORK, IT IS IMPORTANT THAT YOU CLOSE DOWN........

.....SO THAT YOU DO NOT REMAIN OPEN TO ANY NEGATIVE ENERGIES AROUND YOU.

c'mon kitty stop messing about

CLOSING DOWN IS A SIMPLE EXERCISE

YOU CAN DO IT AS A VISUALIZATION, BY CLOSING DOWN YOUR CHAKRAS AND THEN PUTTING ON YOUR PSYCHIC PROTECTION.

EXERCISE — CLOSING DOWN

1 FIND A QUIET SPACE WHERE YOU WILL NOT BE DISTURBED.

2 SIT DOWN OR LIE DOWN AND CLOSE YOUR EYES. BEGIN TO FOCUS YOUR ATTENTION ON YOUR BREATH.

3 ### INHALE
AS YOU BREATHE IN, IMAGINE BREATHING IN A WHITE LIGHT, BRINGING CALMNESS TO THE BODY AND MIND. FEEL THIS CALMNESS WASH THROUGH THE BODY WITH THE IN-BREATH.

4 ### EXHALE
AS YOU EXHALE, RELEASE ANY TENSIONS, WORRIES AND ANXIETIES FROM THE DAY. VISUALIZE THEM LEAVING THE BODY ON THE OUT- BREATH.

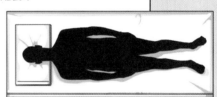
CALMNESS

5 AS YOU BEGIN TO FEEL CALM...

DRAW YOUR ATTENTION TO YOUR CROWN CHAKRA...

NOTICE A PURPLE FLOWER AS IN THE OPENING-UP EXERCISE.

IMAGINE CLOSING THE PETALS OF THE FLOWER, THEN PLACE A GOLDEN BALL OF LIGHT OVER THE CLOSED CHAKRA.

YOUR CROWN CHAKRA IS NOW CLOSED AND PROTECTED.

6 MOVE DOWN TO YOUR THIRD EYE. VISUALIZE AN OPEN BLUE FLOWER. IMAGINE DRAWING THE FLOWER BACK INTO A TIGHT BUD.

WITH THE THIRD EYE

IMAGINE PLACING A GOLDEN BALL OF LIGHT OVER THE CHAKRA TO PROTECT IT.

CLOSE THE CLAIRVOYANT THEATRE SCREEN THAT WE OPENED UP TO ACCESS OUR PSYCHIC SIGHT. VISUALIZE DRAWING THE CURTAIN CLOSED OVER THE SCREEN AND CLOSING DOWN YOUR CLAIRVOYANCE.

7 MOVE DOWN TO YOUR THROAT CHAKRA. VISUALIZE THE OPEN BLUE FLOWER OVER YOUR THROAT.

8 IMAGINE DRAWING THE PETALS CLOSED, SEEING THE BLUE FLOWER TIGHTEN AND GO BACK INTO BUD.

THEN AS BEFORE, PLACE A BEAUTIFUL BALL OF GOLDEN LIGHT OVER THE CHAKRA TO PROTECT IT.

9

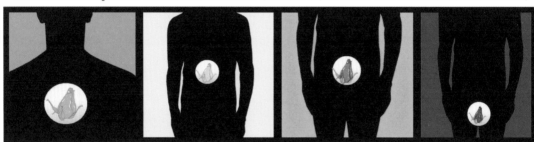

10 AT THE HEART CHAKRA VISUALIZE AN OPEN GREEN FLOWER. DRAW THE PETALS IN AND CLOSE THE FLOWER. THEN PLACE A GOLDEN BALL OF LIGHT OVER THAT CHAKRA. CONTINUE TO WORK DOWN THROUGH THE CHAKRAS.

CLOSING SOLAR PLEXUS, SACRAL PLEXUS, BASE CHAKRA

11 IMAGINE LOOKING AT YOURSELF FROM ABOVE. YOU WILL SEE EACH OF YOUR CHAKRAS IS CLOSED AND PROTECTED BY THOSE BEAUTIFUL BALLS OF GOLDEN LIGHT.

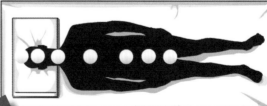

NOW

YOU ARE SAFELY CLOSED DOWN. YOUR ENERGY CENTRES ARE PROTECTED.

NOTE

AFTER CLOSING DOWN, IT IS ADVISABLE TO PUT ON YOUR PSYCHIC PROTECTION. THIS WILL PREPARE YOU ENERGETICALLY TO GO BACK INTO THE WORLD AND DO YOUR NORMAL EVERYDAY THINGS.

GROUNDING

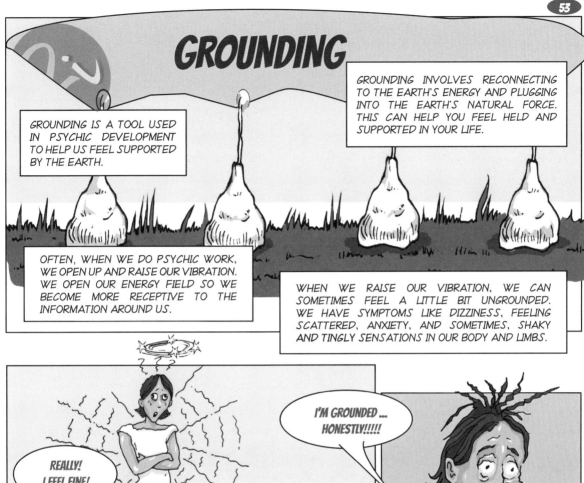

GROUNDING IS A TOOL USED IN PSYCHIC DEVELOPMENT TO HELP US FEEL SUPPORTED BY THE EARTH.

GROUNDING INVOLVES RECONNECTING TO THE EARTH'S ENERGY AND PLUGGING INTO THE EARTH'S NATURAL FORCE. THIS CAN HELP YOU FEEL HELD AND SUPPORTED IN YOUR LIFE.

OFTEN, WHEN WE DO PSYCHIC WORK, WE OPEN UP AND RAISE OUR VIBRATION. WE OPEN OUR ENERGY FIELD SO WE BECOME MORE RECEPTIVE TO THE INFORMATION AROUND US.

WHEN WE RAISE OUR VIBRATION, WE CAN SOMETIMES FEEL A LITTLE BIT UNGROUNDED. WE HAVE SYMPTOMS LIKE DIZZINESS, FEELING SCATTERED, ANXIETY, AND SOMETIMES, SHAKY AND TINGLY SENSATIONS IN OUR BODY AND LIMBS.

REALLY! I FEEL FINE!

NOT LONG NOW!

I'M GROUNDED ... HONESTLY!!!!!

THIS IS ESPECIALLY TRUE FOR VERY SENSITIVE PEOPLE, WHO CAN BE EASILY OVERWHELMED BY THINGS AND BECOME UNGROUNDED.

THEREFORE, IT IS VERY IMPORTANT

FOR ANYONE DOING PSYCHIC WORK, OR ANYONE WHO IS HIGHLY SENSITIVE, TO HAVE A REGULAR DAILY PRACTICE OF GROUNDING.

GROUNDING IS ACHIEVED THROUGH A NUMBER OF WAYS.

ONE WAY OF GROUNDING IS TO SIMPLY GO OUTSIDE, TAKE OFF YOUR SHOES, AND FEEL THE EARTH UNDERNEATH YOUR FEET!

LOOKIN' GOOD!

YES, MUCH BETTER!

THE BEST WAY TO GROUND FOR PSYCHIC WORK IS THROUGH A SIMPLE VISUALIZATION PROCESS

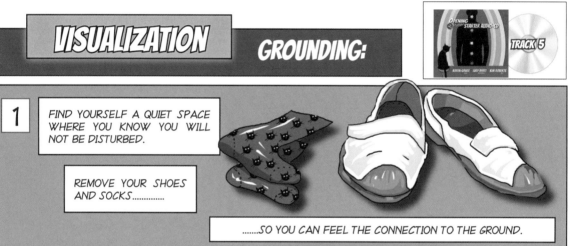

VISUALIZATION

GROUNDING:

TRACK 5

1 FIND YOURSELF A QUIET SPACE WHERE YOU KNOW YOU WILL NOT BE DISTURBED.

REMOVE YOUR SHOES AND SOCKS..............

........SO YOU CAN FEEL THE CONNECTION TO THE GROUND.

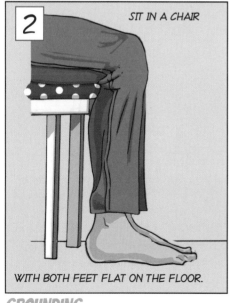

2 SIT IN A CHAIR

WITH BOTH FEET FLAT ON THE FLOOR.

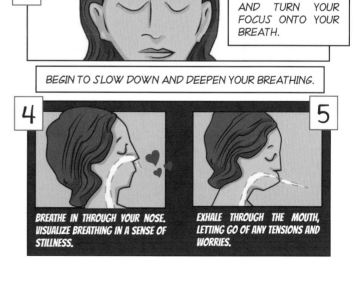

3 CLOSE YOUR EYES AND TURN YOUR FOCUS ONTO YOUR BREATH.

BEGIN TO SLOW DOWN AND DEEPEN YOUR BREATHING.

4 BREATHE IN THROUGH YOUR NOSE. VISUALIZE BREATHING IN A SENSE OF STILLNESS.

5 EXHALE THROUGH THE MOUTH, LETTING GO OF ANY TENSIONS AND WORRIES.

GROUNDING

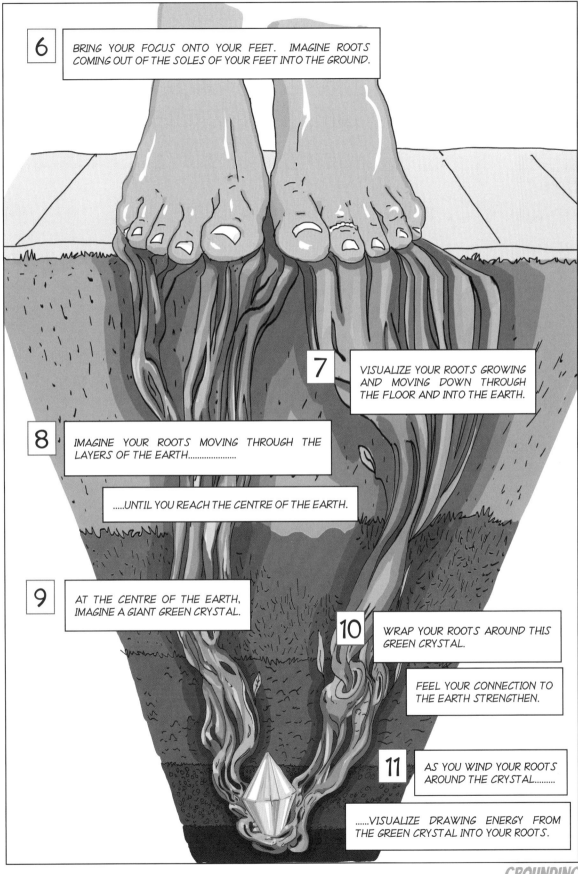

GROUNDING

IMAGINE IT CLIMBING UP THE ROOTS

UNTIL YOU BEGIN TO FEEL IT TOUCHING THE SOLES OF YOUR FEET.

12

ALLOW THE ENERGY TO FLOW UP THROUGH YOUR FEET.

13 INTO YOUR ANKLES AND UP YOUR LEGS.

14 ALLOW YOURSELF TO FEEL THE CONNECTION OF THE EARTH FLOWING INTO YOUR BASE CHAKRA. ALLOW THIS ENERGY TO MOVE UP FROM THE BASE CHAKRA INTO THE SACRAL CHAKRA AND THEN INTO THE SOLAR PLEXUS.

15 KEEP MOVING THIS ENERGY UPWARDS, THROUGH THE HEART CHAKRA AND THROAT CHAKRA, THEN UP INTO THE THIRD EYE.

16 FROM THE THIRD EYE, BRING THIS ENERGY UP INTO THE CROWN CHAKRA.

AT THE CROWN CHAKRA, ALLOW THE ENERGY TO FLOW UP AND OUT OF THE CHAKRA. VISUALIZE IT MOVING OUT OF THE CROWN AND CASCADING LIKE A FOUNTAIN DOWN EITHER SIDE OF THE BODY.

17 AS THE ENERGY FLOWS DOWN AROUND YOU AND REACHES YOUR FEET, VISUALIZE THIS ENERGY MOVING UNDERNEATH YOU, CREATING A CIRCLE OF ENERGY THAT FLOWS BACK UP THROUGH THE CHAKRAS, OUT OF THE CROWN AND BACK INTO THE FEET AGAIN.

INTO THE BASE CHAKRA

INTO THE SACRAL CHAKRA

INTO THE SOLAR PLEXUS

INTO THE HEART CHAKRA

INTO THE THROAT CHAKRA

INTO THE THIRD EYE

INTO THE CROWN CHAKRA

GROUNDING

18

FEEL THE CONNECTION THAT YOU HAVE WITH THE EARTH. FEEL THE EARTH ENERGY HOLDING YOU AND FLOWING THROUGH YOUR CHAKRAS AND ENERGY FIELD. KNOW YOU ARE PERFECTLY GROUNDED AND SUPPORTED BY THE EARTH'S ENERGY.

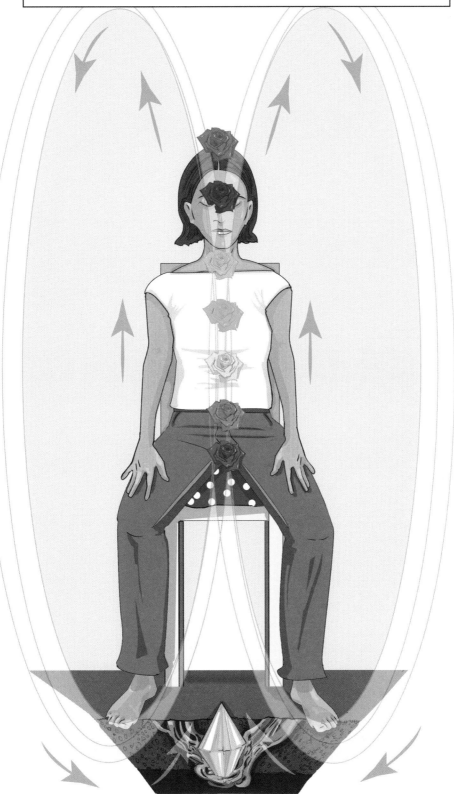

GROUNDING

NOW YOU HAVE COVERED THE BASICS, YOU KNOW HOW TO:

- OPEN UP
- USE PSYCHIC PROTECTION
- CLEAR YOUR ENERGY
- CREATE YOUR SACRED SPACE
- CLOSE DOWN

PSYCHICALLY

PSYCHICALLY WE USE OUR INTUITION TO PICK UP INFORMATION FROM OUR SURROUNDING ENVIRONMENT. WE BEGIN TO SENSE INTO THINGS AND FEEL INTO THE ENERGIES OF PEOPLE AND PLACES AROUND US.

INTUITIVELY

INTUITIVELY YOU WILL LEARN TO PICK UP INFORMATION USING ALL OF YOUR SENSES. INFORMATION WILL COME IN THROUGH WHAT YOU SEE, WHAT YOU FEEL, WHAT YOU HEAR AND WHAT YOU THINK. THESE ARE KNOW AS THE 4 'CLAIRS'.

CLAIRVOYANCE

CLAIRVOYANCE IS CLEAR SEEING.

IT INVOLVES USING THE GIFT OF SIGHT TO SEE THINGS THAT ARE GOING ON AROUND YOU PSYCHICALLY.

A CLAIRVOYANT MAY SEE SOMETHING MANIFEST PHYSICALLY IN THE ENVIRONMENT OR THEY MAY SEE IT MORE SUBJECTIVELY IN THEIR MIND'S EYE,

MOUSE BEING EATEN BY THE CAT!

CLAIRAUDIENCE

CLAIRAUDIENCE IS CLEAR HEARING.

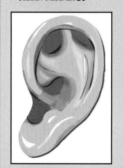

IT INVOLVES USING THE GIFT OF HEARING TO HEAR THINGS THAT ARE GOING ON AROUND YOU PSYCHICALLY. SOMEONE WORKING WITH CLAIRAUDIENCE WILL GATHER PSYCHIC INFORMATION THROUGH HEARING. THEY MAY HEAR THE SOUND EXTERNALLY OR THEY MAY HEAR IT AS A VOICE INSIDE THEIR HEAD, AS IF IT WERE THEIR OWN VOICE.

CLAIRSENTIENCE

CLAIRSENTIENCE IS CLEAR FEELING.

IT INVOLVES USING THE GIFT OF FEELING TO DISCOVER WHAT IS HAPPENING AROUND YOU PSYCHICALLY.

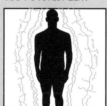

SOMEONE WHO IS CLAIRSENTIENT WILL PICK UP INFORMATION FROM PLACES AND PEOPLE THROUGH THEIR FEELINGS. AN EMPATH WILL PICK UP PEOPLE'S FEELINGS AS IF THEY WERE THEIR OWN. BEING CLAIRSENTIENT THEY INTUITIVELY KNOW WHAT IS GOING ON WITH THAT PERSON THROUGH THEIR FEELINGS.

CLAIRCOGNIZANCE

CLAIRCOGNIZANCE IS CLEAR KNOWING.

NO...IT'S NOT SAFE OUT THERE..I JUST KNOW SOMETHING'S NOT RIGHT!

IT USES THE GIFT OF CLEAR THOUGHT AS A WAY TO ASCERTAIN PSYCHIC INFORMATION ABOUT PEOPLE AND PLACES. SOMEONE WHO IS CLAIRCOGNIZANT CAN PICK UP INFORMATION THROUGH A SENSE OF KNOWING, AND IT IS THROUGH THIS SENSE OF KNOWING THAT THEY ARE ABLE TO MAKE THEIR PSYCHIC PREDICTIONS.

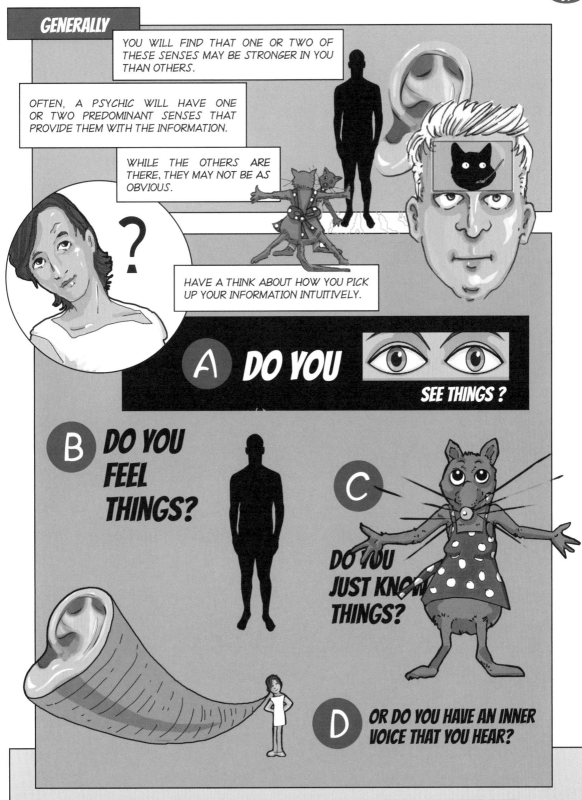

GENERALLY

YOU WILL FIND THAT ONE OR TWO OF THESE SENSES MAY BE STRONGER IN YOU THAN OTHERS.

OFTEN, A PSYCHIC WILL HAVE ONE OR TWO PREDOMINANT SENSES THAT PROVIDE THEM WITH THE INFORMATION.

WHILE THE OTHERS ARE THERE, THEY MAY NOT BE AS OBVIOUS.

?

HAVE A THINK ABOUT HOW YOU PICK UP YOUR INFORMATION INTUITIVELY.

A DO YOU SEE THINGS ?

B DO YOU FEEL THINGS?

C DO YOU JUST KNOW THINGS?

D OR DO YOU HAVE AN INNER VOICE THAT YOU HEAR?

YOU MAY ALREADY KNOW HOW YOU WORK INTUITIVELY.

BIOGRAPHIES

KIM ROBERTS WRITER

IS A PSYCHIC CLAIRVOYANT AND HEALER WITH 16 YEARS' EXPERIENCE IN PSYCHIC READINGS AND TAROT. SHE IS A FULLY QUALIFIED REIKI MASTER AND NLP PRACTITIONER.

KIM WORKS AS BOTH A READER AND A TEACHER, AND HAS RUN NUMEROUS HEALING AND PSYCHIC DEVELOPMENT WORKSHOPS OVER THE PAST FEW YEARS IN THE UK.

KIM RUNS AN ONLINE PSYCHIC DEVELOPMENT GROUP FOR CELEBRITY PSYCHIC MICHELE KNIGHT ON A WEEKLY BASIS. KIM HAS A B.A.HONS DEGREE IN ENGLISH AND PSYCHOLOGY AND IS A WRITER INTERESTED IN EXPLAINING AND DEVELOPING THE EASY UNDERSTANDING OF ENERGY AND THE NATURE OF HEALING.

LUCY BYATT ILLUSTRATOR

IS A PSYCHIC ARTIST WITH NEARLY 30 YEARS' EXPERIENCE IN SPIRITUAL TRAINING, HEALING, REIKI, MEDIUMSHIP AND PSYCHIC DEVELOPMENT. SHE HAS TAKEN MANY COURSES AT THE COLLEGE OF PSYCHIC STUDIES IN LONDON AND HAS WORKED AS A PSYCHIC ARTIST WITH VARIOUS COMPANIES, DOING READINGS, DEMONSTRATIONS AND TALKS.

LUCY ALSO WORKS WITH AUTISTIC CHILDREN AND MENTORS CHILDREN IN SCHOOLS IN 'DANGER OF EXCLUSION', AS WELL AS STUDENTS INTERESTED IN PSYCHIC AND COLOUR DEVELOPMENT, LUCY HAS FACILITATED A NUMBER OF WORKSHOPS AT THE ISBOURNE FOUNDATION IN CHELTENHAM, TEACHING COLOUR AND PSYCHIC ART.

LUCY GRADUATED WITH A B.A. HONS 1ST DEGREE IN FINE ART FROM GOLDSMITHS ART COLLEGE, AND HAS AN M.A. IN SCULPTURE FROM THE UNIVERSITY OF GLOUCESTERSHIRE. SHE HAS MANY YEARS' EXPERIENCE AS A FREELANCE ILLUSTRATOR AND GRAPHIC DESIGNER WORKING FOR NUMEROUS BUSINESSES. LUCY HAS EXHIBITED HER SCULPTURES AT THE FLORENCE BIENNALE.

LUCY AND KIM BEGAN WORKING TOGETHER IN 2007 AND, THROUGH TRANCE CHANNELLING WITH THEIR GUIDES, **OPENING2INTUITION** CAME INTO EXISTENCE.

ACKNOWLEDGEMENTS

THANK YOU

OPENING2INTUITION WOULD LIKE TO THANK THEIR SPIRIT GUIDES FOR PROVIDING DETAILED CHANNELLED INFORMATION FOR THIS BOOK.

WE WOULD LIKE TO THANK KAREN GRACE FOR COMING ON BOARD AND GETTING INVOLVED WITH OPENING2INTUITION. SHE HAS PROVIDED SOME SPECTACULAR MUSIC AND VOCALS FOR OUR CD. KAREN HAS ALSO PUT IN NUMEROUS LENGTHY SKYPE CONFERENCE CALLS AND IS A VALUABLE MEMBER OF OUR TEAM.

WE WOULD LIKE TO THANK CAROLYN FINLAY FOR PROOFREADING THIS BOOK. THANK YOU. YOUR MANY HOURS DOTTING I'S AND CROSSING T'S OVER THE WONDERS OF THE TELEPHONE WERE INVALUABLE AND ENJOYABLE.

WE WOULD LIKE TO THANK CHRISTINE MITCHELL FOR LENDING US HER MUSICAL EAR TO LISTEN TO THE FINAL CHECKS FOR THE CD. THANK YOU, YOUR INPUT AND TIME WAS MUCH APPRECIATED.

WE WOULD LIKE TO THANK KATHRYN TRAYNOR, OLWEN TRINGHAM, DENISE RUTTER AND LIZ HILLIES FOR TAKING TIME OUT OF THEIR BUSY SCHEDULES TO PROOFREAD THE BOOK AND LISTEN TO FINAL CHECKS AROUND THE CD.

WE WOULD LIKE TO THANK OUR READERS FOR BUYING THE BOOK, AND WE HOPE THAT OUR WORK ENABLES YOU TO OPEN UP TO YOUR INTUITION IN NEW AND EXCITING WAYS.

WE WOULD ALSO LIKE TO THANK OUR FAMILIES AND FRIENDS, WHO HAVE BEEN PATIENT AND UNDERSTANDING OF THE WORK AND TIME WE HAVE NEEDED TO DEDICATE TO MAKING THE COMPLETION OF THIS BOOK POSSIBLE.

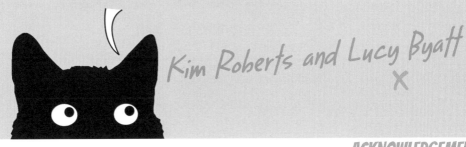

Kim Roberts and Lucy Byatt
X

OPENING 2 intuition

WWW.OPENING2INTUITION.COM

OPENING2INTUITION, GUIDEBOOK 1
"PSYCHIC DEVELOPMENT, THE BASICS"
IS A CHANNELLED BOOK.

OUR AIM IS TO PROVIDE A SIMPLE,
FUN, CREATIVE, SAFE WAY TO OPEN
UP YOUR INTUITIVE ABILITIES.

OTHER GUIDEBOOKS AVAILABLE IN THIS SERIES:

BOOK 2:
MEETING AND
WORKING WITH
YOUR
SPIRIT GUIDES

BOOK 3:
DISCOVERING
YOUR PAST LIVES

AND ALSO THE STARTER AUDIO-CD:

8 TRACKS

ALL OUR BOOKS AND OUR STARTER CD ARE AVAILABLE
FROM YOUR LOCAL BOOKSHOP OR FROM

WWW.FINDHORNPRESS.COM

WHERE YOU WILL ALSO FIND DOWNLOADABLE
ELECTRONIC VERSIONS (EBOOKS AND MP3,
RESPECTIVELY).

WEBSITE/COURSES

WEBINARS

MENTORING

DEVELOPMENT CIRCLES

ONLINE

COURSES

1:1 TEACHING

VIDEOS **WORKSHOPS** CDS

IF YOU ARE INTERESTED IN DEVELOPING YOUR INTUITION FURTHER, PLEASE COME AND VISIT OUR WEBSITE.

WWW.OPENING2INTUITION.COM

ON OUR WEBSITE YOU WILL DISCOVER MANY ADDITIONAL RESOURCES, INCLUDING ONLINE TEACHING COURSES AND MP3 DOWNLOADS.

WE WILL ALSO KEEP YOU UP TO DATE WITH THE PROGRESS OF OUR NEXT BOOK, TEMPLATES, DOWNLOADS AND CDs IN THE **OPENING2INTUITION** SERIES.

COME AND JOIN US AT THE CREATIVE PLACE TO DEVELOP YOUR INTUITION.

FINDHORN PRESS

Life-Changing Books

Consult our catalogue online
(with secure order facility) on
findhornpress.com

For information on the Findhorn Foundation:
findhorn.org